Funny Stuff

How Great Cartoonists
Make Great Cartoons

Phil Witte | Rex Hesner

Prometheus Books

Essex, Connecticut

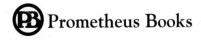
Prometheus Books

An imprint of Globe Pequot, the trade division of
The Rowman & Littlefield Publishing Group
4501 Forbes Blvd., Ste. 200
Lanham, MD 20706
www.rowman.com

Distributed by NATIONAL BOOK NETWORK

British Library Cataloguing in Publication Information Available

Library of Congress Cataloging-in-Publication Data
Names: Witte, Philip, 1957- author. | Hesner, Rex, 1952- author.
Title: Funny stuff : how great cartoonists make great cartoons / Philip Witte and Rex Hesner.
Description: Lanham, MD : Prometheus, [2024] | Includes bibliographical references. | Summary: "Funny Stuff is a tribute to a unique art form: the single-panel gag cartoon. It looks at why so many of us enjoy cartoons, and what makes for a great cartoon. Authors Phil Witte and Rex Hesner consider how cartoonists can present a complex or odd scenario that we immediately grasp, and what enables us to 'get' the humor in a flash"—Provided by publisher.
Identifiers: LCCN 2023040889 (print) | LCCN 2023040890 (ebook) | ISBN 9781633889804 (cloth) | ISBN 9781633889811 (epub)
Subjects: LCSH: American wit and humor, Pictorial. | Caricatures and cartoons—United States. | Cartoonists—United States.
Classification: LCC NC1426 .W58 2024 (print) | LCC NC1426 (ebook) | DDC 741.5/6973—dc23/eng/20231206
LC record available at https://lccn.loc.gov/2023040889
LC ebook record available at https://lccn.loc.gov/2023040890

♾️™ The paper used in this publication meets the minimum requirements of American National Standard for Information Sciences—Permanence of Paper for Printed Library Materials, ANSI/NISO Z39.48-1992

Contents

Foreword

BOB MANKOFF

Let me take a wild guess—you have a soft spot for cartoons. You wouldn't be holding this book if you didn't, and I wouldn't have penned this foreword if I hadn't dedicated my career to them. We're kindred spirits, you and me. If life were a cartoon, we'd likely be sharing a panel.

The cartoons I'm alluding to are those that filled countless issues of the *New Yorker* during my four-decade tenure there as a cartoonist and cartoon editor. They bear the rather inelegant moniker of "single-panel gag cartoons." Yet, when done right, there is nothing inelegant about them. They epitomize a graceful fusion of word and image, giving rise to laughter and thought.

That said, most people, after laughing, don't give cartoons a second thought. Thankfully, Phil Witte and Rex Hesner, the authors of *Funny Stuff*, aren't most people. They're my kind of people: cartoon aficionados who understand that true enjoyment comes from a blend of delight and appreciation.

Just as music courses enhance our appreciation by dissecting melody, rhythm, and harmony, *Funny Stuff* accomplishes a similar feat for gag cartoons. Through a curation of more than 100 cartoons, equal parts edifying and funny, you're enrolled in

Courtesy of Benjamin Schwartz.

"It sort of makes you stop and think, doesn't it."

a first-rate course in cartoon appreciation. Not only do Phil and Rex decipher the mastery behind the art, but the maestros themselves, legendary *New Yorker* cartoonists like Roz Chast, Jack Ziegler, Peter Vey, Mick Stevens, Sam Gross, and a cadre of emerging legends, also share their unique perspectives and anecdotes. So prepare to view the world through a cartoonist's lens—a place where the ordinary becomes extraordinary, and the comedic potential of life is brought into sharp relief. Once you see it that way, you'll never look back.

Acknowledgments

We greatly appreciate the support and encouragement that we received from Bob Mankoff, who told us a few years ago, "You guys should write a book." Thanks goes to the good folks at CartoonStock, source of most of the cartoons in this book. We also thank Jonathan Kurtz of Prometheus Books, who wisely selected *Funny Stuff* for publication, and our agent, Leigh Eisenman of Wolf Literary Services, who knows her way around a lengthy contract. Our deepest appreciation goes to the cartoonists who generously gave their time to help us produce this book; we couldn't have done it without them. We're also grateful to the family of the late Jack Ziegler for granting us permission to quote from his unpublished memoir. Last, we thank gag cartoonists everywhere for making the world funnier, both ha-ha funny and strange-funny.

Introduction

This book is a tribute to a unique art form: the single-panel gag cartoon. A "gag" in the comedy universe is a joke or funny idea. So, the gag cartoon is an illustrated funny idea. The format consists of one drawing, typically with a brief title or caption, with a humorous intent.

Something so simple can have a powerful effect on us—so much so that we tape them on refrigerator doors or office walls and email them to friends. And why? We believe something magical happens when a cartoon succeeds. A connection is made with the reader that is both emotional and intellectual. How does that happen, and what makes for a great cartoon? Those are a few of the questions we explore in this book. In doing so, we've tried not to crush the humor out of the cartoons under the weight of excess analysis. If you prefer your humor crushed, give Freud's *Jokes and Their Relation to the Unconscious* a read. Not funny.

Should cartoons be taken seriously? Can one experience greater joy by gaining a deeper understanding of the craft of cartoons? Are there definitive answers to these questions? Yes and no, and it depends. But most of all, we'd like to share more than 100 great cartoons that illustrate the issues and themes we address in this book and offer concise commentary. We'll talk about what makes the cartoons work, offer insights into the underlying humor, and provide a backstage look at the profession itself.

Before proceeding further, a few words on what *not* to expect.

This isn't a how-to book per se, but it may help beginning cartoonists better understand how great cartoons are created and remind established cartoonists of concepts they already apply subconsciously. Of course, if a beginner cartoonist becomes world-famous after reading this book, we won't hesitate to take partial credit.

This isn't a collection of the greatest cartoons of all time, but it does include great cartoons that illustrate the points we make. Funnier cartoons may have served our purposes better, but, hey, there are a lot of cartoons out there, and we can't keep track of all of them.

This book includes the work of many great cartoonists but certainly not all of them due to space constraints. Who knows, maybe we'll write a second volume.

This book doesn't address multi-panel cartoon strips or editorial cartoons, but certain sections of this book, such as our discussion of the creative process, also apply to them. We love *Calvin and Hobbes*, but sequential cartoon art has a logic and pace that demands a separate analysis. Likewise, editorial cartoons are a category unto themselves.

A final note of explanation:

This book includes many cartoons originally published in the *New Yorker*, but that's not to say all cartoons in that magazine are great or even that all of the cartoonists whose cartoons appear in it are great, but it does say that many great cartoons have been featured in that magazine.

Almost all of the cartoons in this book can be found on cartoonstock.com, a compendium of hundreds of thousands of cartoons available for lease. Readers of this book who discover cartoonists they like will find many more examples of their work on the site. Cartoonists who we mention but whose cartoons we did not include also have cartoons on the site.

But enough . . . Is an introduction to a book of cartoons even necessary? What we really need is a cartoon to segue into the first chapter. Mick Stevens says it all with a caveman-themed cartoon about, well . . . cartooning.

CHAPTER ONE
Single-Panel Cartoons
UNDERSTANDING THE MAGIC

WHAT'S SPECIAL ABOUT THE SINGLE-PANEL CARTOON?

The single-panel cartoon, or gag cartoon, is unique in the world of humor. The reader engages with a cartoon differently than with any other medium. Its format, generally a small monochrome drawing with a brief caption, pulls the reader into the drawing first. The drawing conveys the circumstances that set up the gag. With the scenario in mind, the reader then takes in the caption—if there is one—and the moment is at hand. If the one-two combination of image and words succeeds, a small detonation occurs in the reader's mind, resulting in a smile, a chuckle, or an outright guffaw.

The single-panel cartoon also occupies a unique place in the world of graphics. It compresses a cartoonist's view of life into a single drawing. In one image, the cartoon presents a scene with contradictory components or offers an observation expressed in a novel way. When we make sense of the scenario, usually by untangling an amusing rearrangement of reality, the result is a successful cartoon. And unlike multi-panel cartoons, which usually consist of a setup in the initial panels followed by the punchline in the final panel, the single-panel has to pull together all elements of the gag into one drawing.

No other form of humor delivers the goods with such immediacy. The communication between cartoonist and reader is almost instantaneous. The reader accepts the cartoon's peculiar logic, and the cartoonist rewards the reader with an unexpected

"I thought we agreed you weren't going to work at home."

twist of reality. Worlds freely collide, for example, in this gem by Peter (P. C.) Vey.

Let's briefly break down the components of the gag cartoon, all of which we'll explore more deeply in subsequent chapters.

FROM FUNNY IDEA TO FUNNY CARTOON

THE GAG

Every cartoon starts with a funny idea, or gag, that can be depicted as a drawing. Gag writing requires looking at the ordinary and transforming it into something completely different yet still recognizable, just as Picasso could see a bicycle seat and handle-bars and transform them into a bull's head. Coming up with lots—as in thousands—of original gags worthy of drawing and submitting for publication requires a skill that

few possess. Having that ability or gift or form of madness is magical in itself. It's all part of the creative process, which we'll cover in this book.

The cartoonist must have a mind that can freely associate unlike things and find the common element that unites them. But that is only the first step. The transformed thing or scene that eventually becomes a cartoon must be funny. There's no formula for funny, but the gag will more likely succeed if it presents a scenario that twists reality in a refreshing and unexpected way. The twist can be gentle, as is common for observational, conversational cartoons, or, in the case of the most absurd cartoons, the twist can be so extreme as to squeeze out all recognizable signposts of real life.

Humor has many forms, including observational, satirical, dark, whimsical, absurd, ironic/sarcastic, and slapstick, among other types, which we'll explore in the next chapter. The type of humor favored by a cartoonist will turn on that cartoonist's personal inclinations, something the cartoonist—or the cartoonist's therapist—can best describe. We'll get into that in chapter 9, titled "Twisted: The Psyche of the Cartoonist." Great cartoons also have a point of view, a way of looking at the world, that characterizes the humor. The cartoonist's personality is, in a sense, an element of the cartoon.

THE DRAWING

Inventing hilarious, original gags is an indispensable talent, but drawing them is another matter. Cartoon art is a specific type of illustration skill. The art must present a scene and characters that can be grasped immediately, so that even the most bizarre image can be comprehended. In the words of Jack Ziegler, a cartoonist who masterfully combined an uncluttered artistic style with absurdist humor:

> [A cartoon] is a snippet. In general, it depicts a single moment in the lives of the protagonists—the best cartoons providing enough of a thumbnail history so that the reader knows everything he needs to know about what went on before and what will probably transpire afterwards. This is all provided in the drawing by the demeanor, clothing, room furnishings, etc., and is so inherent in the whole concept of cartooning that the reader remains unaware of what is automatically intuited about these characters.

Unlike multi-panel cartoons, the single-panel has to pull together all elements of the gag into one drawing. Ziegler's ice cream cartoon does just that—and without a caption. It's quite a trick to pull off.

More than most cartoonists, Ziegler dared to present bizarre situations as the premise of his cartoons, yet he found the common thread that allowed the humor to come through. This bold defiance of, or even rebellion against, expectations blew the doors open for crazier cartoons. Other cartoonists, notably his friend Mick Stevens and more recently Zach Kanin, followed Ziegler's path.

THE CAPTION

The Ziegler ice cream cartoon belongs in the category of cartoons—those without captions—that are the exception. Most single-panel cartoons feature one character saying something. Getting the caption just right is another skill required of cartoonists. The caption must put across the humor in a few words that leave no doubt as to the message conveyed. Word choice, word placement, and caption length are among the topics we'll discuss.

In this cartoon by Eric Lewis, the caption has great import as the famous last words of a character realizing that the end is near. Cartoons suffused with irony, such as this one, serve as excellent vehicles for exposing our frailties and foibles.

"I should have bought more crap."

WHICH IS MORE IMPORTANT, THE DRAWING OR THE GAG?

The consensus in the cartooning world is that a great drawing won't save a weak gag, but a great gag can survive mediocre artwork. Great cartoon drawing doesn't mean beautiful works of art—but it also doesn't mean wacky-looking characters with overwrought expressions. Great cartoon drawing means effective artwork that pairs well with the gag's type of humor. It does more than convey information; it propels the cartoon to greater comic heights by adding interest, emotion, and delight.

The artwork should draw us in and evoke curiosity. It can achieve that by being charming or strange or pleasantly familiar. An unconventional style, even a naive one, can be intriguing. Above all, it must not be boring. A unique, recognizable artistic style that conjures a specific type of humor sets the great cartoonist apart from the wannabes.

SURFACE MEANING AND SUBTEXT

Great cartoons have a surface meaning and a subtext. The surface meaning is the literal reading of the cartoon and may have no connection with everyday reality. The subtext is the actual subject of the cartoon. It's what the cartoon is riffing on. A cartoon's subtext is based on a common experience or shared belief or knowledge. The reader must be familiar with the subtext to "get" the gag.

Surface meaning and subtext may have no obvious relation to each other. Take a pirate cartoon, for example. On the surface, a pirate captain may be addressing his crew in a cartoon, but beneath the surface, the subtext could be something else entirely. It may be human relations or monetary policy or whatever the cartoonist wants to comment on. The pirate scenario is the setup, but the gag lies in the subtext. The reader must be able to connect the literal reading of the cartoon and the subtext for the cartoon to work. Discovering the best setup to put the gag over is a critical element to creating a successful cartoon.

Here's an example by Carolita Johnson that doesn't require deep digging to arrive at the subtext. The age-old conflict between men and women plays out

"Is that all you can think about?"

between household pets with incompatible bedtime goals. Despite the hearts on the kitty's sleepwear, she has no time for her overeager bedmate.

CULTURAL REFERENCES

For a cartoon to work, the cartoonist and viewer must share a certain body of knowledge. People won't understand a cartoon if they don't know what it refers to, either on the surface or implied in the subtext. Without that knowledge, the viewer can't make a connection between what's depicted and the point of the cartoon. A person from a different culture, education, or upbringing may not have the information to unlock the funny.

Take for example Bob Mankoff's cartoon on this page. One must be familiar not only with Rodin's widely parodied *The Thinker* but also his sculpture *The Kiss* to fully appreciate the gag.

A cartoon's subject matter may be a blind spot in any particular person's knowledge, whether it's popular culture, current events, or the latest discovery in plasma physics. A cartoon that features a phone book may puzzle a young reader, while one that centers on a popular phone app may be a head-scratcher for the older set. A cartoon not landing effectively may be due to a cartoonist assuming too much of the audience.

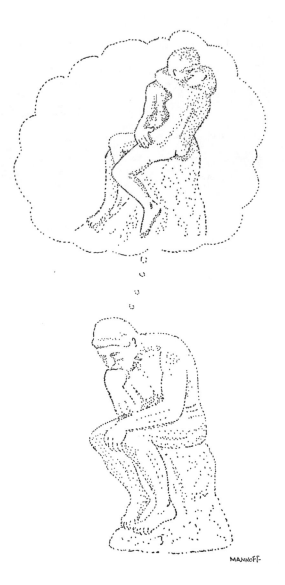

INCONGRUITY: THE KEY TO CARTOON HUMOR

Cartoons reflect our lives, but they don't mirror them. Instead, they contain incongruous elements that create conflict. When the incongruity is part of the drawing, we call it visual incongruity. The dog should not be chairing a business meeting. The pirate has no business in an elementary school class. A medieval king would not be shopping at a modern grocery store. The image in each case may be amusing in itself, but the cartoon must resolve the incongruity. In most cases, it does that through the caption—words spoken by a character that explain why, within the logic of the cartoon, the apparent incongruous elements are actually compatible. And, for the cartoon to succeed, the caption must unify the conflicting elements in a novel, clever way.

Joe Dator, a brilliant cartoonist, offered this insight:

I feel that the cartoon should involve something happening that could not possibly happen, but which has a kind of truth to it. There should be a give-and-take between the truth and the implausibility. If those two things are going on at the exact same time, and they're both equal in weight, then the brain has a conflict that it has to resolve, and it can only resolve it through laughter.

It also makes cartoons more fun to draw if there's something strange and weird and absurd and surreal in the cartoons.

Voilà!

"It's only until spring."

Incongruity alert! What's a bear doing in the bedroom? The caption resolves the incongruity by implying that bears, given the absence of local caves, might show up in bed from time to time for an extended snooze. In other words, what appears to be an incongruity is actually quite normal, at least from the bear's point of view. Conflict resolved. An excellent incongruous cartoon.

But not all cartoons have out-of-place elements in the drawing, no visual incongruity. The drawing may depict a perfectly normal, everyday scene. For these cartoons, the caption *creates* the incongruity instead of resolving it. The cartoon character says something that's at odds with the drawing or is not typical of what someone would say in similar circumstances. These cartoons

turn on a different type of incongruity—where the incongruity is between the drawing and the caption. Joe Dator has something to say about them as well: "If it's just two people talking, I like at the very least for them to be saying something that no one would ever say in real life, because it would be either offensive or rude or just strange."

To highlight the difference between graphical incongruity and verbal incongruity, consider another bedroom scene, below, also by Dator.

No one saw that caption coming, especially given the ordinary setting. A reader could sustain comedic whiplash from the two-sentence caption. We accept the first sentence as relatively normal, only to be startled by the second line. The pathway

"Come on, let's have kids. Next week you can pick a restaurant."

to the humor lies in the absurdity of the non-sequitur, one that pairs a momentous life decision with a trivial one. This wholly original gag is equal parts absurd and dry, like the recipe for a perfect cartoon martini.

At first glance, the drawing doesn't contribute much to the humor. It simply presents an intimate setting for a discussion about procreation. Upon closer consideration, we see how the image and caption work together. The man has put his book down, giving his wife a sidelong look. Although Dator's style flattens the couple's facial expressions, we can still read the man's skepticism. On the other hand, the woman directly addresses her husband with an oddly constructed proposition, highlighting the disparity between the unremarkable setting and the wildly surprising caption.

WHAT'S FUNNY ABOUT IT?

Suppose you "get" the cartoon, in the sense you understand the gag, but you just don't think it's funny. Of course, certain types of humor appeal to certain types of people. Irony plays better in some cultures, and not at all in others. Sarcasm may come across as perplexing or downright rude. Slapstick appeals to a segment of audiences worldwide, but can degenerate into a cheap laugh. Both understated humor and absurd humor often appeal to the same crowd, while leaving others unmoved. The British may lay claim to the most vibrant world

of gag cartoons in print, with the United States not far behind, but other countries are cartoon deserts—and sadder for it, in our opinion.

Race, gender, and ethnic background may also figure into how one reacts to a cartoon. Age may be a factor not only in understanding a cartoon but also whether the reader finds it funny. Cartoons about the elderly, for example, may seem a lot less funny as we gray. Gag cartoonists take the sensitivities of others into account, especially in the current climate. Tastes and standards change with the times, a point that cartoonist and cartoon editor Bob Mankoff may have had in mind with this cartoon:

"Hey, Eddie, wanna hear a joke that's offensive now, in bad taste two years from now, funny in eight, and no one gets in twenty?"

If you have a favorite cartoonist, it's probably because that cartoonist's sense of humor aligns with yours, a subject we explore in the next chapter, "Amusing to Zany: Types of Humor."

CHAPTER TWO

Amusing to Zany

TYPES OF HUMOR

In this chapter we'll consider seven broad categories of humor applicable to cartoons: observational, satirical, dark, whimsical, absurd, ironic/sarcastic, and slapstick. These categories have applications beyond cartoons, of course, but we'll try to stay in our lane—and if we decide to change lanes, we'll signal you, the reader.

Cartoonists have their own way of seeing the world. This point of view shapes their approach to humor. A cynical cartoonist will likely produce cartoons that are darkly humorous. A cartoonist with a more charitable view of humankind may address our foibles less harshly. Generally, the process happens unconsciously. The veteran cartoonist gravitates toward an approach to humor that, for that cartoonist, feels natural and produces good results.

First, a few prefatory remarks. *Ahem.* By classifying cartoons according to type of humor, we are not plucking them up with a tweezer and inserting them into specimen jars to be put on a dusty shelf for exhibit, like a nineteenth-century taxonomist at a natural history museum. That would kill the funny. Cartoons must be free to breathe and frolic in the light of day. We may pin category names on them, but they are at liberty to shake them off, and, rascals that they are, pin them on other cartoons. Some cartoons warrant multiple labels. Other cartoons defy categorization, or constitute an inter-label species of cartoon. Who are we to challenge how they define themselves?

We also acknowledge that library shelves at universities are jam-packed with weighty tomes that analyze humor in its many manifestations in art and literature. We have not read any of them or even seen them for that matter, but we're pretty sure they exist. Our approach is refreshingly not academic.

Disclaimers dispensed, we turn to our categories of cartoon humor.

SATIRICAL HUMOR

Most cartoonists—and standup comedians for that matter—are social critics, at least to some degree. They poke fun at the failures of our institutions, hypocrisy of politicians, foolishness of bosses, and unfairness of life in general. Pretty much anything that civil society rests on is fair game. Satirical humor can be biting or gentle, but there must be an element of truth laid bare in the cartoon. We are forced to acknowledge that truth. Sounds grim, so how can it also be funny?

We consider that question through the cartoon by Paul Noth. The well-groomed wolf with a self-satisfied look on his face is, of course, a stand-in for a politician, and the sheep are voters. The unapologetic proclamation on the billboard—note the American flag pin on the wolf's lapel, indicating that he is a patriotic carnivore—sits well with one of the two sheep who even

"He tells it like it is."

bothers to consider the sign. The other sheep are oblivious; they can be seen as unengaged citizens and non-voters. It's also noteworthy that the wolf is not dressed in sheep's clothing, so there's no issue of mistaken identity.

Why would a sheep speak with admiration of a wolf, its natural predator? The answer, as anyone who enjoys the cartoon knows, is that voters will support a candidate they feel they can relate to, no matter how irrational that feeling. Here, the feeling is wrapped in an easy political cliché repeated by the sheep speaking the caption. Voters, like the sheep in the cartoon, often vote against their own interests.

The cartoon is critical of unthinking voters, voracious politicians, and our political system as a whole. Even though it's not a political cartoon of the type found on a newspaper's editorial page, Noth's cartoon, published in the *New Yorker* during the election year of 2016, is a scathing commentary on U.S. politics, presented in a wickedly funny way. The outrageous political slogan, the wolf's knowing smile, and the dopiness of the sheep combine perfectly to create a humorous drawing with a serious message.

Satirical cartoons need to make their point without being pedantic. The element of humor distinguishes the satirist from the crank. The humor can be harsh or subtle, even sneaky, as it mocks parents, teachers, medical and legal professionals, and the institutions representing them.

OBSERVATIONAL HUMOR

Many cartoonists, again like standup comedians, rely on observational humor. Comedians who preface their jokes with "Ever notice . . . ?" are using observational humor. In a sense, all humor is observational humor in that it's based on something observed and considered, even if the cartoonist reshapes the subject. But here we're referring to a type of cartoon in which typically not a lot is happening in the drawing, except for one person saying something—an observation of some sort—to another person.

The observational cartoon has a point, but the humor is not as pointed as the humor in a satirical cartoon. The subject is likely to be an everyday matter, but seen from a different perspective. The setting is familiar, such as a restaurant, home, or office. This type of cartoon was more common in years past, and often featured a character at a cocktail party making an unintentionally funny remark. Because the drawing doesn't typically present an unusual situation, the caption must deliver the humor.

Edward Koren was a cartoonist whose humor fits into this category. His scratchy line and beak-nosed characters are familiar to longtime readers of the *New Yorker*. His cartoons are peopled by urban types, whether enjoying the city's attractions or spending a weekend in the country. The humor gently mocks the characters, whose observations are just slightly inappropriate, as in this cartoon:

"This is the same music my fitness instructor plays for our abdominal crunches."

DARK HUMOR

Cartoons that rely on dark humor tiptoe near—and sometimes over—boundaries of social acceptability. In fact, they often flout the very existence of boundaries. Dark humor may offend, outrage, or otherwise ruffle the feathers of polite society. A good cartoon that relies on dark humor can be shocking, but not for the sake of being shocking. As with every cartoon, it must have a subject and a point of view. At the same time, without such a transgressive element, the cartoon would lack its comedic punch. It's part of the gag. Cartoons of this type go beyond pointing out hypocrisy or unfairness. The target is often the bedrock principles of civilization. What could be funnier, right? Executed well, it can also be a powerful cartoon.

Some cartoonists, like edgy standup comedians, find satisfaction in tackling uncomfortable subjects, even at the risk of alienating a portion of their audience. Certain subjects, however unpleasant, are irresistible for cartoonists. Take death, for example, a common theme in dark cartoons. Think of all the cartoons featuring the Grim Reaper,

the personification of death dating back to the Middle Ages. We leave it to psychologists to explain the connection between death and humor. Regardless, we note that the Reaper, despite his forbidding appearance— he's usually depicted as a scythe-wielding skeleton in a hooded cloak—is often portrayed in cartoons as silly or inept.

David Borchart combines death and disaffection between married couples in a single, dark cartoon. Here, the wife makes a game of helping the slow-witted specter of death locate her husband. The Reaper has already checked out the other room, indicated by the partially obscured door, and even searched an end table drawer and behind a pillow—all amusing details that the cartoonist includes.

In sharp contrast with dark humor is . . .

"Getting warm. . .warmer."

WHIMSICAL HUMOR

The whimsical cartoon is fanciful and light. It can touch on the strange but not the perplexing. Its subjects are uncontroversial, and the treatment of its subjects is nonjudgmental. Even if the gag is occasionally challenging, the cartoon will meet you halfway. A successful whimsical cartoon will bring the reader a warm sense of delight but fall short of a laugh-out-loud response.

The wonderful work of John O'Brien, including his illustrations for children's books as well as cartoons, epitomizes whimsy. A pizza cutter becomes, of all things, a unicycle, creating a highwire as it slices through the pizza. The chef performs in an elegant nightclub-like setting with well-dressed guests arranged at tables around the pie. The scene captures the moment the chef has tossed the pizza dough high above the crowd.

"Howard, I think the dog wants to go out."

Is there a caption to explain how these impossible elements have coalesced? No. In fact, there is no gag in the traditional sense. We are simply asked to let go and enter the artist's fantasy world.

Pets figure prominently in whimsical cartoons. This classic cartoon by Arnie Levin is a splendid example. It's more conventional than the O'Brien cartoon, with a drawing that's funny by itself. A lesser cartoonist might be tempted to overdraw the image, but Levin's wavery line and casual ink wash add to the whimsy. The dog, placed in the center, is drawn with greater precision and detail. His formal dress and posture, with paws resting on the walking stick, cape draped over the tuxedo, carnation in jacket, and of course, silk top hat on his furry head, sets up the gag before we get to the caption. The gag is fairly obvious, turning on the meaning of "going out," but the graphical execution elevates the cartoon to a classic.

IRONIC AND SARCASTIC HUMOR

Irony is a common device in literature and other forms of storytelling. In cartoons, the humor usually stems from a character's unintentionally ironic behavior. We laugh at how unaware the character is. Sarcasm, irony's nasty cousin, is weaponized humor. The speaker intentionally says the exact

"Oh. Wow. Another sonnet."

opposite of what is meant, often as a form of criticism. Because it can be sharp, sarcasm is a device that the cartoonist must wield with care.

Poor Will, his priceless literary gift seems to have fallen on deaf ears. Trevor Spaulding's caption makes her ladyship's sarcasm clear with three perfectly placed periods.

ABSURD HUMOR

Absurd humor is humor without boundaries; often there is nothing to "get." The absurdity itself is what's funny. While cartoons in general often contain incompatible elements, they are usually resolved in the caption. Cartoons we classify as absurd either don't fully resolve the incongruity or don't resolve it at all.

The cartoonist whose work consistently escapes the gravitational force of logic and spins headlong into another galaxy is Edward Steed, one of the most original cartoonists to appear in decades. Neither his gags nor his artwork is encumbered by convention. The most absurd of

"Do you mean good, or good for a pumpkin?"

his cartoons don't even follow a twisted logic. No character is a stand-in for the reader, and no clue is offered to explain the weirdness. Why not a pumpkin painter, and a defensive one at that?

The drawing style boasts a primitive savagery, as if the cartoonist himself were enraged as he drew the cartoon. Bob Mankoff, who nurtured Steed's work early on, once asked him if he could draw better. "Not really," was Steed's modest reply.

Regardless, his work has won the admiration of more conventional cartoonists, who appreciate his boldness and wild creativity. Steed's humor is tinged with madness—in a good way.

Reactions to absurd cartoons, like Steed's pumpkin-as-artist, can vary dramatically. Some may find it bewildering or just plain silly. Others may feel frustrated trying to make sense of a cartoon. "Am I missing something here?" is an understandable response. Certainly, the more absurd the cartoon, the more difficult it is to explain why it's funny.

Here we would like to offer an homage to the enormously popular and influential gag cartoonist Gary Larson, creator of *The Far Side*. Unfortunately, the famously reclusive cartoonist doesn't allow the reprinting of his cartoons or we would have featured them here. Suffice it to say that *The Far Side* was a breakthrough cartoon that embraced absurdity for fifteen years since its 1980 inception. The conservative world of syndicated dailies was reluctant to carry it at first, but readers quickly caught on.

Larson's simply but hilariously drawn characters—women with beehive hairdos, dopey men, overstuffed children, and bevy of animals—continue to delight readers, even though Larson walked away from *The Far Side* in 1995. It paved the way for other outré cartoonists, most notably Dan Piraro, creator of the aptly named *Bizarro* syndicated cartoon. Both Piraro and Larson, it should be noted, credited B. Kliban as a key influence, both for his surreal humor and drawing style.

DRY HUMOR

Characterized by understatement, dry humor is a subtle form of cartoon humor. Dry humor seeps into the brain, where it marinates for a few moments in a pleasurable way. We're not immediately sure what motivates the character to take a low-key approach. By contrast, a bug-eyed cartoon character shouting with a wide-open mouth leaves no doubt as to what's in that character's mind. The bug-eyed character has its place in the Sunday funnies, but that's an area we'll leave for someone else to explore.

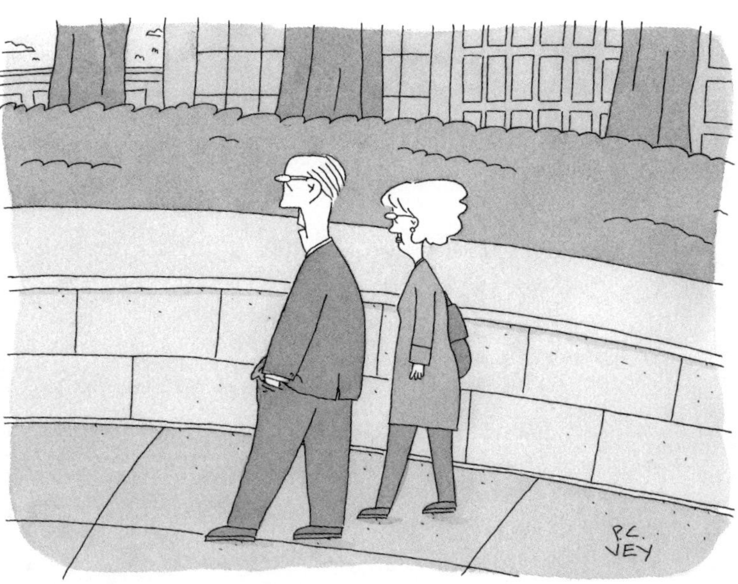
P.C.
VEY

"Those once-in-a-lifetime events are beginning to add up."

Dry humor is well-suited to everyday scenarios. In the Peter Vey cartoon (previous page), we can barely detect the expressions on the faces of this elderly couple as they stroll away from us; a character's flat affect typifies dry humor. In this example, something profound is wrapped in understatement. No need to shout. Adding an exclamation point would diminish the impact of the character's observation.

CYNICAL HUMOR

The cynical cartoonist holds a funhouse mirror up to the worst of human behavior. Take for example, Bob Mankoff's cartoon about love and marriage. That's the subject of this cartoon, not what it depicts. Mankoff takes aim, literally, at the institution of marriage. (Whether or not this middle-aged couple is married, we can safely assume they're in a committed relationship. After all, they share a couch.) If this cartoon is a statement about relationships, particularly but not exclusively between men and women, why even bother trying?

The message is grim and the image violent, but the husband's magnificent understatement lightens an otherwise bleak scene. Mankoff uses exaggeration to amp up the antagonism between the man and woman. Discord is baked into the scene as the man casually answers the phone amid the marital mayhem. The caption gives new meaning to a common reply to a phone inquiry. Visually the cartoon is quite effective as well. The path of the bullet directs our attention to the speaker. The sofa, taking up most of the space, is like an immovable third character.

"As a matter of fact, you did catch us at a bad time."

SLAPSTICK

Whether a pie in the face, slipping on a banana peel, or anvils falling from the sky, slapstick depicts exaggerated physical violence. Saturday morning cartoons on TV imprinted entire generations with this form of broad comedy. Venerable cartoonist Sam Gross plumbs prehistory for the oldest known slapstick incident.

Gross chose to focus not on the invention of the wheel—a common cartoon setup—but on an unexpected consequence of having round, rolly things on a cave floor. Brilliant as the caveman inventor was, he did not foresee the hazard they posed to the unwary. By presenting a slapstick scenario, the cartoonist has reduced one of the great accelerators of civilization to a household nuisance.

With so many types of humor to choose from, coming up with a few hundred or thousand great cartoon ideas is probably a snap, right? Wrong, of course. How cartoonists follow their creative paths is explored in the next chapter.

CHAPTER THREE
Funny How That Works
THE CREATIVE PROCESS

"He's done it all. There's nothing left to draw."

THE SPARK OF INSPIRATION

"Where do you get your ideas?" is the question most frequently asked of cartoonists. After all, as Tom Toro's caveman classic suggests, hasn't it all been done before? It's a surprise to most people that the magazine editors at the *New Yorker* expect regular contributors to submit about ten cartoons every week. They're equally surprised to learn that their favorite syndicated cartoonists, such as Dan Piraro (*Bizarro*) and Dave Coverly (*Speed Bump*), must produce one cartoon daily for years on end. Above all, each cartoon must be original, acceptable to the editors, and funny to the readers. So, how do cartoonists keep coming up with fresh ideas?

The answer is simple. Cartoonists get their ideas from the same place that all good ideas come from: some blend of conscious and subconscious thought. Accessing that place, however, can be tricky, perplexing, and sometimes distressing. The stimulus that triggers an idea could be a snatch of conversation overheard (or misheard) while waiting in line for coffee, a news report or weather forecast, a magazine article, an ambulance siren, a beautiful sunset, a garbage truck making its rounds—in other words, all of the same stimuli that the average person experiences. These stimuli, combined with dreams, childhood memories, fears, anxieties, and—believe it or not—joyful moments, are the yeast that yields a fully fermented cartoon. For example, David Sipress, whose cartoons often have

an autobiographical element, told us that his ideas spring from what makes him angry or scared or what he finds ridiculous. See his airport cartoon on the opposite page.

But how do cartoonists open themselves up to these potential sources of inspiration? Jack Ziegler had this routine to prime the creative pump:

> I'd begin drawing around these notations, letting my mind drift, and doodle whatever did or didn't make sense. There were a lot of times when it seemed there wasn't any thinking involved at all. It was pure daydreaming. If the pencil wasn't moving, I'd just sit there staring off into space. To the casual observer, I might have appeared catatonic. After as much as three hours of this head-spinning burst of activity I'd take a break. Some days I'd have nothing to show for this process, but others might produce as many as five workable—though not necessarily good—ideas.

Other cartoonists have their own particular approaches. Harry Bliss gets up, makes coffee, and spends time reading and writing in bed before he begins cartooning. Kaamran Hafeez peruses the *New York Times* and the *New Yorker* for a turn of phrase that has comic potential. In Frank Cotham's house, the TV is tuned to CNN, providing a familiar soundscape that puts him into a creative frame of mind. Peter Vey's background soundtrack is NPR or music to "keep my fore-brain occupied." William Haefeli lets the stream of ideas ebb and flow. "I try to keep it organic," he said. Liana Finck finds inspiration while taking long train rides. Other cartoonists take a stroll to

"No, this is correct—you're both in 28-B. We no longer offer individual seats."

recharge their neurons. Mick Stevens sees a link between cartooning and music. An avid jazz saxophonist, Stevens has said, "The music keeps my mind active, [so] when I get to the drawing board it's running."

The pressure to produce is felt particularly by syndicated cartoonists, who are contractually required to create a fully realized cartoon 365 days a year, come what may. Dan Piraro looks at great cartoons by other cartoonists for inspiration.

The resulting cartoons, he told us, are completely unrelated to the cartoons that inspired him. Dave Coverly stressed the importance of reading broadly on many topics as a generator of ideas. "The creative process doesn't begin with humor," he told us. "It begins with subject matter."

When it comes to inspiration, Edward Steed lets his cartoons do the talking. In our example, a studious-looking canine attempts to connect with the muses. Unfortunately,

possible cartoons. He estimated that he rejects 90 percent of what he jots down, but he may come back to, say, notebook number thirty-two many years later and find the key that unlocks a great cartoon.

More mysterious is the cartoon that emerges in the cartoonist's mind without any conscious thought about, well, anything. When this happens, the cartoon creator can't explain how it happens, only the euphoria of the experience. In a conversation with his wife that veteran cartoonist David Sipress recounts in his wonderful and poignant memoir *What's So Funny?*, he described it this way: "[W]hen an idea comes to me like this, it's as if it happens to me, almost as if I had nothing to do with it, like it came out of nowhere—a gift from the cartoon gods. . . . [E]very time it happens like that, I get this rush—an intense physical pleasure that feels like pure joy, and it's like fireworks going off in my brain."

We've all been struck with a sudden mental jolt. An idea pops into our heads about something we've had in the back of our minds for days. This jolt often happens when we're relaxed, not thinking about anything in particular. A morning shower is a common place for these magical occurrences. Cartoonists must always be prepared for that moment when inspiration strikes—especially with a deadline looming—regardless of the circumstances, and be able to record it for later cartoon illustration. "I'm pretty much always thinking about ideas, and the antennae are always

as stubbed-out cigarettes and a blank page attest, his efforts are futile, a common affliction for any artist. As we've seen, cartoonists employ various methods to prime the pump during a creative drought. Perhaps our humorous hound can take Coverly's advice about subject matter to find his voice. Check out his keyboard—he's only a "woof" away from his magnum opus.

Many cartoonists never leave the house without some method of preserving ideas. Jack Ziegler carried a clipboard wherever he went for jotting down notes on whatever happened to cross his mind. John O'Brien is another inveterate note-taker. Over the decades, he has filled more than fifty notebooks with ideas and thumbnail sketches that he later considered for

out," said Mick Stevens. "Because I've been doing it for so long, it's just part of my life now so much that I'm automatically thinking that way." His cartoon above says it all—and without a caption.

WHICH COMES FIRST: THE CAPTION OR THE DRAWING?

The second most common question that cartoonists hear is, "Which comes first: the caption or the drawing?" Because some cartoons have no captions, the question more accurately phrased is whether the gag or the drawing comes first. There are basically two camps: writers and sketchers, with a fair amount of overlap between them. For the writers, the funny idea comes first, but that's an oversimplification. Generally, the writers simultaneously have a good sense of what the drawing will look like. For most cartoonists, the setting of the gag will be one that's familiar to cartoonists and readers: a bar, living room, office, or flame-filled Hades. The cartoonist then draws a version of the setting that supports the joke elements and caption. Simple, right? Not so! Cartoonists can spend hours arranging and rearranging the visual aspects of the drawing, not to mention perfecting the caption's phrasing.

The writers usually jot down ideas as they come to them and return to their ideas later to draw them. Cartoonist and best-selling author Roz Chast, with a foot in both camps, has an idea box, a large shoebox to be precise, into which she puts scraps of paper and partially sketched ideas. Over a two- or three-day period, she selects the ideas she likes. She told us:

It's not efficient. Some of them go through the wash, and then the best ideas I've ever had are probably lost in a dryer somewhere. It is quite insane because sometimes I pull out a handful and I look at the stuff I've written, and I think, "Was I asleep? What am I writing here?" It's just bananas. But you never know.

Roz shared with us the recent contents of her idea box:

Courtesy of Roz Chast.

We can't say whether the weasel ever graduated from a sketch on a scrap of paper to a cartoon.

William Haefeli jots down about twenty-five ideas on a sheet of paper and crosses them off one at a time as he draws them. When he gets down to five ideas he snips them out with a pair of scissors and puts the strips of paper into an envelope. When he runs low on ideas, he sifts through the envelope for a likely subject. It works for him.

Often an idea is too ill-formed to be the basis of a cartoon. The cartoonist will mentally play with the idea, trying several different ways to present it or refine it. If the idea can't be hammered into a solid gag, it must be rejected.

If the idea has potential, it moves to the drawing stage. Typically, that may mean making a few preliminary sketches. If an element of the drawing is tricky to draw—bicycles, for example—or if the cartoonist wants to make sure a detail is accurate—how did French aristocrats dress in the eighteenth century?—the internet is a ready source for a photo reference. Perhaps the cartoonist will sketch a few studies of gestures or facial expressions. If no one else is around or is willing to act as a model, a selfie taken in front of a mirror can help the cartoonist convey an emotion. Cartooning is not for the self-conscious.

A few elements the cartoonist must consider in composing the drawing are: where and how characters should be positioned, what the characters should look like, how much detail to include, and how the drawing and gag can best work together to elevate the humor. Perspective lines and the point of view must be taken into account. Because people "read" cartoons from left to right, the movement of the cartoons should flow in that direction. Even for experienced cartoonists, this is a trial-and-error exercise. Erasing happens.

William Haefeli can knock off a sketch in ten or fifteen minutes. A finish takes him up to two weeks. As you look closely at his cartoons in subsequent chapters, you'll appreciate the care he lavishes on the details. His talent is astonishing and, to his fellow cartoonists, humbling. John O'Brien can complete one of his intricately drawn pieces in anywhere from a few hours to a few days. Marisa Acocella can turn out a sketch in five minutes, but it takes her two days to complete a finish. The trick is to give the finished drawing the liveliness of a sketch. Anxiety can cause a cartoonist to freeze up, making a too-perfect drawing appear lifeless.

When an idea occurs to Kaamran Hafeez, a frequent contributor to the *New Yorker* and the *Wall Street Journal*, he has a sense of how to set up the gag visually, but on some level he also has in mind how great cartoonists might approach the task. His touchstones are the works of Jack Ziegler, Robert Weber, Mischa Richter, and Charles Saxon, among others. He then draws the cartoon in his own style, developed over many years. Below, Hafeez takes us through the stages of cartooning, from rough sketch to finished drawing, a process that takes him three days. (The *New Yorker* accepts rough sketches from veteran cartoonists because the editors know vets will come through with a publishable final product.)

Day 1—Pencil sketch

He begins with a light pencil sketch using simple shapes to lay out the composition (first image).

He creates the illusion of 3D space by building up the structure of the characters, furniture, and landscape (second image). For added realism, he finds photos on the internet of objects and uses them as a basis for his drawings "to give the viewer the feeling that they are really there in that cartoon space," in his words.

More detail is added in pencil to prepare for inking (third image).

Courtesy of Kaamran Hafeez.

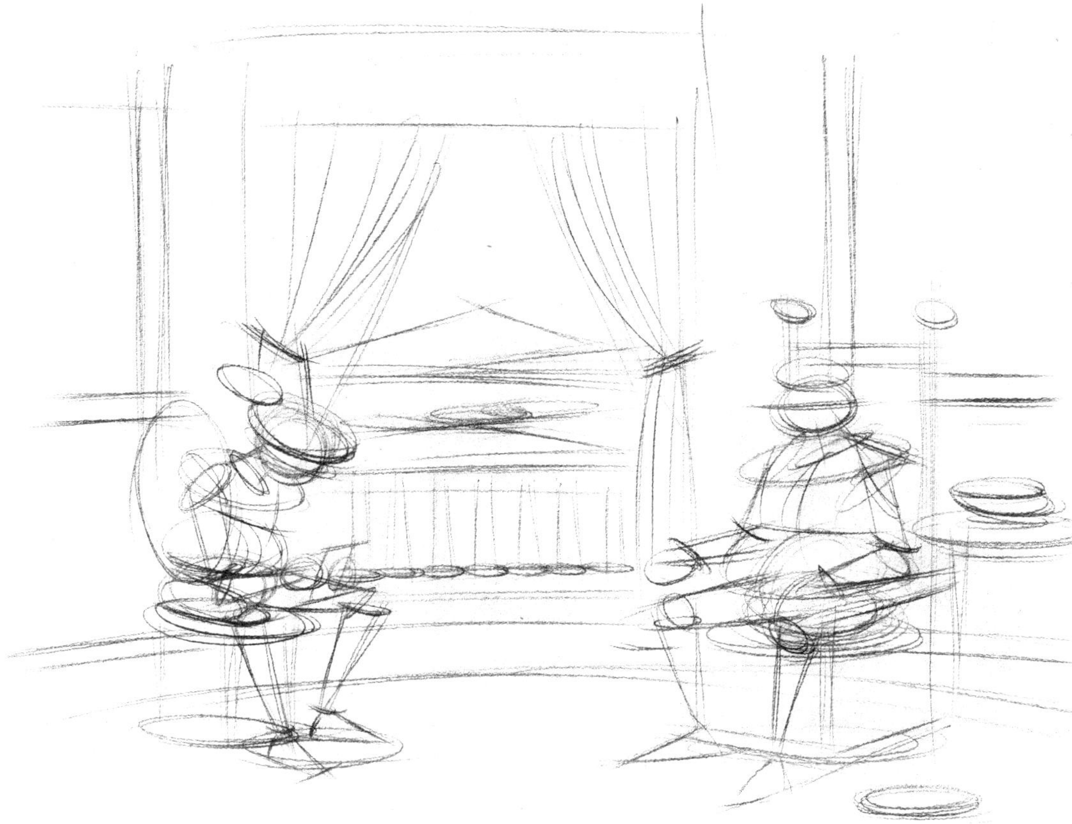

Courtesy of Kaamran Hafeez.

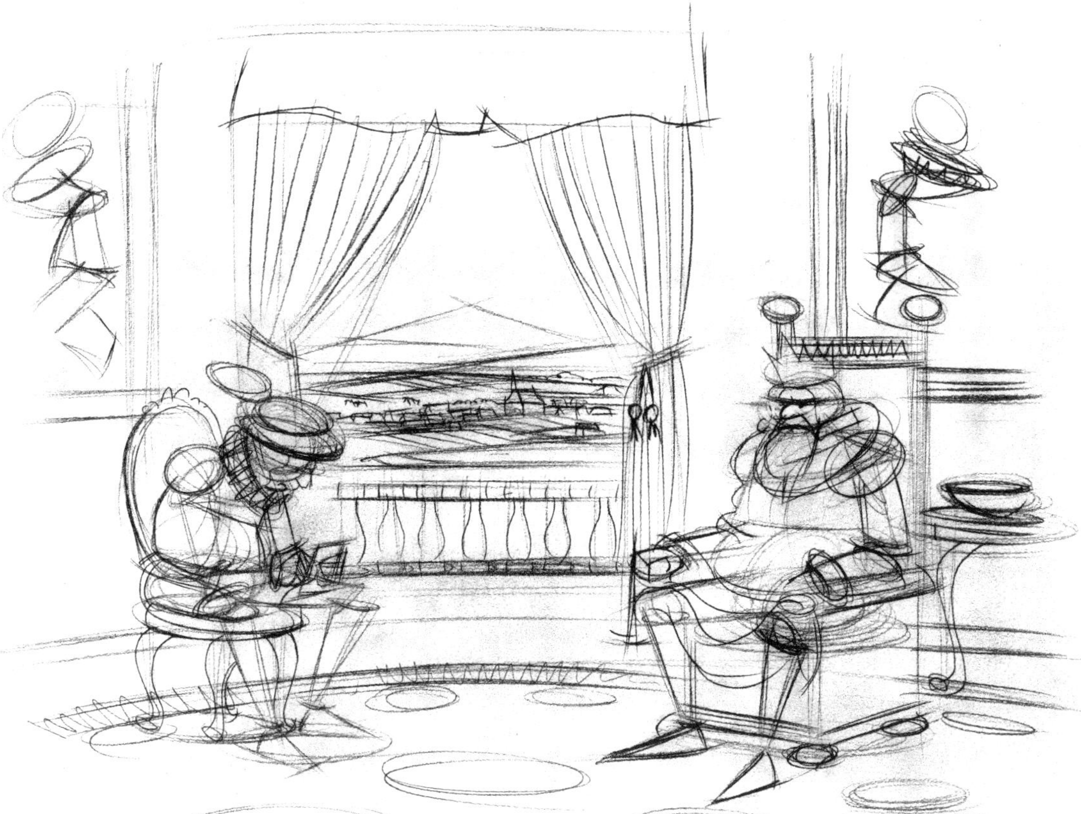

Courtesy of Kaamran Hafeez.

Courtesy of Kaamran Hafeez.

Day 2—Inking the penciled art.

This is the most unforgiving step. If he inks a bad line, he tosses the drawing and starts over. "It takes a great deal of focused energy, but is very gratifying when I get it right," he said. "The key is to involve my imagination. I dream it into being by imagining how I want it to be. I lead with my imagination and, inevitably, the brush follows" (fourth image).

Day 3—Shading and light.

"Before I begin adding shading, I spend a lot of time staring at the line art and imagining/visualizing where the shading will go. I try to imagine a way to create the illusion of rays of light contrasted with deep shadow." He then darkens the shadowed areas and the characters' clothing.

The result is a warm, beautifully realized cartoon, perfectly balanced, with a strong contrast between interior and exterior and light and dark, with elements that are either detailed or merely suggested—all done with black ink and wash (fifth image).

Sketchers are less common than writers. They usually come to cartooning from the art world or have some formal art training (as do many writer-type cartoonists). Peter

"The peasants are mercilessly ridiculing you online."

Vey, for example, usually starts sketching without an idea where it might lead. A drawing that begins with a couple sight-seeing on a mountaintop may morph into a couple stranded on a cliff. The gag may come later, or not at all. Similarly, for Harry Bliss, the drawing often comes before the caption. "I'll imagine a narra-tive that led up to the drawing and that continues after the fact," Bliss said, "so you develop a backstory based on that drawing."

Frank Cotham starts each day with a blank piece of paper. Sometimes he doodles and comes up with an image of a medieval scene, like the date-challenged soldier climbing the castle parapet.

"The siege was yesterday."

Or Cotham will draw a husband and wife sitting on the front porch of their ramshackle shack—another favorite cartoon setting of his—and hope that the caption magically arrives. Other times, he may hear a bit of conversation that he'll tweak into a gag and come up with a drawing to match it. "Every now and then I'll get up in the morning, sit down, and here I got a blank piece of paper and absolutely no idea whatsoever." That must be a rare occasion because he typically cranks out three fully finished cartoons—not just rough sketches—every day.

Joe Dator, whose cartoons strike the perfect balance between the understated and the absurd, works back and forth between the wording and the drawing. He'll write a sentence, then draw something, which in turn will generate a new sentence. He describes his mental flow as he develops ideas in his sketchbook:

> The real work is not that you get a flash of an idea, and you write it down, and it's done and it's perfect. That's great when that happens. But what's really great is when you get something, but you're not sure what. Then it becomes something else. And you have that wonderful time of sitting down with your sketchbook and working it out. Then you can completely lose yourself in that mindset.

When the well is dry, Dator likes to draw animals, mostly birds because "birds are just fun to draw" and sometimes become the subject of a cartoon. Dator admits that his approach is not efficient.

"After all these years, I've come to accept that there's going to be a certain amount of pain in this job, and that's my lot in life, that's my burden."

John O'Brien, cartoonist and illustrator of over 100 children's books, thinks of gags in terms of the image. He consciously avoids cartoons that require captions, akin to a juggler who has tied one arm behind his back. John generously shared with us two pages from one of his notebooks that illustrate the visual evolution of a cartoon. It began with a chicken on a vertical rotisserie that caught his eye. How could he use that chicken in a cartoon? His first thought was to transform the chicken into a football referee signaling a touchdown. That led to chicken goalposts. Other possibilities include the chicken as a stickup victim or a chicken-shaped beachgoer. He even considered replacing the chicken with a chef on the spit (first sketch).

O'Brien later returned to his sketches, and noticed that the football tailgating sketch reminded him of a foosball table, which in turn resembled a rotisserie grill. The chickens stood in for the soccer figures, and two chefs became the foosball players (second sketch).

The finished cartoon as published does not call to mind a chicken on a spit, but the germ of the idea remains.

Whether a writer or a sketcher or some combination, cartoonists describe the creative frame of mind using terms such as

SPIT
GRILL
GRIDIRON
GOALPOSTS
CHEF ON SPIT
CHEF
FOOD AS PLAYERS
STADIUM
GOALPOSTS TAILGATING

Courtesy of John O'Brien.

STICKS OTHER SIDE
ONE SIDE
FIRST: 3 PLAYERS
SECOND: 2 PLAYERS
SIXTH 3 PLAYERS
ONE SIDE

Courtesy of John O'Brien.

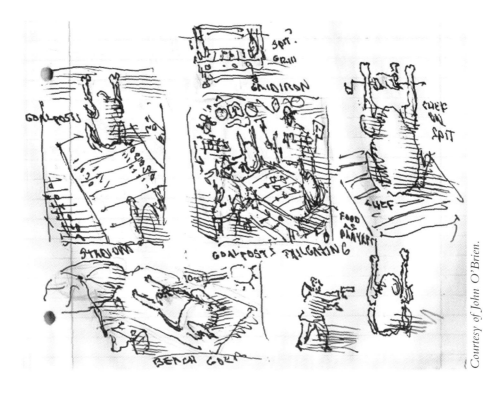

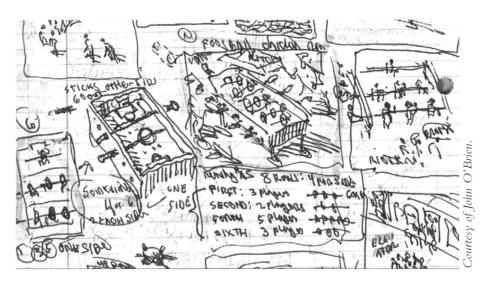

"losing myself," "in the flow," and "day-dreaming," almost as if the ideas arrive involuntarily. Everyday pressing issues inhibit that flow—so you'll forgive cartoonists if they sometimes seem (and, in fact, are) distracted. Even when cartoonists are engaged in other activities, they are receptive to stimuli that trigger an idea. "Part of my brain is always thinking about cartoons," said David Sipress. He told us that even during yoga classes, when the mind is supposed to be in a state of calm, ideas for cartoons may rush into his brain.

Just as important as an open mind is a mind that is unconstrained by what anyone thinks is funny or worthy. Bliss is adamant on this point: "It is nice to get your cartoons accepted, but if you can get past that and just draw for yourself and just try not to give a shit, which I know sounds arrogant, but that's how you have to be." Not all cartoonists, including well-known ones, have that degree of confidence. Even Roz Chast, one of the most successful cartoonists working today, occasionally has her doubts. She told us, "One of the biggest excitements for me is if I do a cartoon, and I think, 'They'll never take this. It's way too personal.' Then, if they take it, that makes my life."

Cartoonists aren't always the best judge of their work. With few exceptions, they can't predict which cartoons will be accepted for publication. The best ones in their opinion often get passed over, while a tossed-off cartoon gets bought. A prime example is the well-known office cartoon by Bob Mankoff shown below.

It was published in 1993 and has been reprinted and ripped off countless times. It served as the title to Mankoff's memoir and even earned him an entry in *The Yale Book of Quotations*. The caption was a line in an actual telephone conversation Mankoff had with a cartoonist—Mankoff described him as "a world-class pain in the ass"—who was being difficult about setting a date to meet. After the conversation, Mankoff said to himself, "Hey, that's a good line," and added it as the caption to a generic office drawing. He included the cartoon with his usual weekly batch of a dozen or more cartoons for the *New Yorker*. "I honestly had

"No, Thursday's out. How about never—is never good for you?"

no idea that cartoon had anything unusual about it, other than it's a quip. . . . It's the kind of thing you might say in Queens when I was growing up." To Mankoff's complete surprise, it became a classic. He added, "That cartoon is a good example of nobody knows anything, except maybe Tina." (Tina Brown was the editor-in-chief of the *New Yorker* at the time.)

For such a famous cartoon, the drawing is unremarkable—just a talking head without another head listening. Moreover, the caption is repetitious; it could have ended with "How about never?" which is how most people remember it. "Is never good for you?" is comedic piling on. But instead of weakening the gag, it amps it up, pushing against our tolerance for sarcasm. The caption is a two-punch punchline.

The most fundamental question is, what sort of mind comes up with so many cartoon ideas? Cartoonists see life through a comedic lens that enables them to imagine a cartoon, just as comedians can turn an everyday experience into a comedy routine. The cartoonist's lens is like a funhouse mirror that distorts reality but not to the extent that the reality is unrecognizable. This altered reality may be presented through the drawing, which could be laughably ridiculous or bizarre to the point of being unsettling, but always has some connection to real life. Or the drawing may accurately present reality, but the caption indicates something is way off. Or both.

WHAT ARE THE ODDS?

Before leaving this chapter, we offer some statistics about the selection process so readers can appreciate the astounding rejection rate that cartoonists endure. In his lifetime, Jack Ziegler created over 24,000 cartoons while selling fewer than 3,200, mostly to the *New Yorker.* Believe it or not, that's a high success rate. Even for regular contributors to that magazine, the rejection rate exceeds 95 percent. Frank Cotham, now one of the regulars, estimated that he submitted somewhere *between 7,000 and 10,000 cartoons* over a period of fifteen years before his first one was okayed. For future cartoon editor Bob Mankoff, the number was about 2,000. Kim Krimstein submitted about 800 cartoons before getting a cartoon published *anywhere,* and it was ten years before his first cartoon appeared in the *New Yorker.* One of the most prolific gag cartoonists of all time, Sam Gross, who continued to draw cartoons until his death at age eighty-nine, sold only a fraction of the more than 33,000 cartoons he produced. Dogged persistence must be part of the cartoonist's skill set.

Coming up with dozens of good gags generally means that the cartoonist weeds out hundreds of meh gags. Recognizing the difference between them is a crucial professional skill. As Dave Coverly observed, "The biggest part of this job is editing." Magazine editors have their own ideas about what's funny, and they seldom tell the cartoonist what those ideas are. And editors change, which can mean a cartoon-ist who once was "in" is now "out."

Adding to all this, the number of publications that buy cartoons has shrunk. The ones that remain have kept their payment rates the same for years and in some cases decreased them. Online publications have sprung up, but most pay a pittance.

Despite almost insurmountable odds, cartoonists continue to produce, many well into old age. Successful cartoonists rarely retire. Like artists who create "fine" art, they cartoon for the love of it.

We close this chapter with words of wisdom from the inimitable Roz Chast:

I feel like I have been astonishingly fortu-nate, because I do not have a plan B. This is really all I've ever done. I've only drawn. I wasn't great at school. I've never worked in an office. I don't have great people skills.

I still have a lot of anxieties. I think about Sam Gross. He's had some very interesting words of wisdom, one of which is, "Just remember, any minute it can all turn to shit." That is sort of my general mindset, that all sorts of different anvils can fall out of the sky at any time.

CHAPTER FOUR

Eureka, It's Funny!

IDEA GENERATION

AT THE LAFF-A-MINIT

With deadlines looming, how do cartoonists generate a batch of original cartoons every week? While some cartoonists do not actively, consciously think of ideas, others take a more structured approach: they mine ideas from well-worn pathways we've dubbed the "Idea Generator." Jack Ziegler, creator of tens of thousands of cartoons, has a wry take on idea generation at his home studio on the previous page.

Typical idea generators are cliché situations, stereotypical characters, characters we know and (mostly) love, personal characters, and lifestyle scenarios. Let's dive deeper into each concept.

CLICHÉ SETUPS

The word "cliché" has a negative connotation. It normally refers to an overused or trite expression, like "happily ever after." However, in the cartooning world, clichés—in the sense of a recurring graphic setup—can serve a useful purpose. Cartoonists know that if a reader doesn't get the joke within a few seconds, the gag is a dud, and the reader will be frustrated. So cartoonists need visual shortcuts to speed up comprehension of their gags.

The cliché setup provides that shortcut, allowing cartoonists to present complex situations in a single frame. Upon seeing an image of Noah's ark, Easter Island heads, or a patient on a psychologist's couch, we need no further explanation. We've seen these images so often that they're instantly recognizable. We make specific associations with these images, which the cartoonist can manipulate to create the gag.

Cartoonists also frequently rely on settings that lend themselves to comic developments. Some settings are commonplace—a courtroom, a doctor's office, or an elementary school, as examples—while other settings are removed from the everyday—a medieval castle or outer space. Other cartoonists choose settings in bars or bedrooms or boardrooms because, in their minds, that's where funny things can happen.

One cliché setup has been a mainstay of the cartoon world for decades: the desert island. Why this setting has endured is a mystery. Do such tiny, precipitation-challenged islands litter the South Pacific? If so, why do castaways end up on them instead of, say, the shores of Tahiti? Despite all that, we frequently find two characters biding their time there, as isolated as Vladimir and Estragon in *Waiting for Godot*.

Sofia Warren executes the required desert island elements: an impossibly small island surrounded by ocean, barefoot castaways in tattered clothing, and the obligatory single palm tree. The drawing (opposite page) tells half the story; the caption relies on the reader's rapid understanding of the visual cliché setup to get the gag.

Given the sheer number of published variations on the desert island cartoon, it's challenging to come up with a new angle. Nevertheless, more than a few undeterred cartoonists continue to rack their brains in

*"I'd say my number–one issue is getting off the island,
and then, after that, probably health care."*

search of a new iteration of this venerable theme. Joe Dator told us that when he came up with a desert island cartoon that no one had thought of before, "that was a great day in my life as an artist."

Other cartoonists avoid clichés as limiting or unoriginal. Indeed, they can be a crutch as much as a tool. Bob Mankoff observed that "they can get to be a little bit incestuous in that they just keep eating their own brain, running after their own tail, until it becomes a particular kind of game." Mick Stevens has conflicting feelings about using these cartoon templates, such as the familiar evolving fish that ventures onto land:

I started trying to get away from the clichés on several occasions and they just sink back in. They just won't go away, like I'm a slave to these things. I thought, "I'll just use them ironically." You can't really tell the difference. The attempt might be ironic, but basically the reader doesn't see the irony. I finally got to the point where I said, "I'm going to draw the last [evolving fish] cartoon." I thought, "That's it, I'm done."

Here's the cartoon he's referring to. It's an example of a meta-cartoon, in which the cartoon itself references a cartoon convention.

"[The *New Yorker*] bought that cartoon," he recalled, "which encouraged me to do more of them." Thus, an ironic cartoon led to an ironic result.

We've mentioned a few common cartoon setups, but there are many more . . . so many more! We've included an appendix of the Top 100 cartoon clichés after the final chapter, and that list only scratches the surface, to use a cliché.

STEREOTYPICAL AND STOCK CHARACTERS

Like clichés, the term stereotype generally carries negative associations about groups of people. And, like clichés, stereotypes are shortcuts. We've all seen stereotyped characters such as the hillbilly, Hollywood producer, or absent-minded professor. Cartoonists wring humor from our concept of these generalized types, regardless of whether they are fair or accurate.

Elisabeth McNair takes aim at stereotypes that children pick up on. Her cartoon works as a good gag, as well as a commentary on whether to bear children. As readers, we don't know if the cartoonist is taking a position on that decision, but stating these options in the plain language

*"You can be the mom. I want to be the family friend
who has plants instead of babies."*

of a child is quite clever. The children are not themselves stereotypes but play at pretending to be them. McNair has an assured graphic style. Notice how the girl on the left, looking nonplussed, protects her doll while her playmate attends to a potted plant, her doll tossed aside.

Cartoonists will insert stereotyped characters into a variety of scenarios. These include, by way of example, prison inmates, mobsters, cowboys, astronauts, preachers, undertakers, and surgeons, not to mention anthropomorphized cats, dogs, and other creatures. Pirates have their proponents. Cartoonist Ken Krimstein explained why in an interview: "They have so many cool parts and things that are wrong with them: eyepatch, hooked hand, pegleg, cool cloaks, nasty beards, big earrings, funky hats, gnarly swords, and parrots on their shoulders. What more could you ask for!"

Cartoon humor occasionally revolves around broad perceptions of characters from different countries. Stereotyping a culture has become less common, fortunately, but a few classic cartoons have played on this convention, such as Michael Crawford's ode to the French:

FRENCH ARMY KNIFE

CHARACTERS WE KNOW AND (MOSTLY) LOVE

Basing a cartoon on a well-known character, whether fictional or historical, quickly draws a reader into the joke. We all hold an accumulation of these characters in our minds. Cartoons based on fairy tales will have a go at Rapunzel, Cinderella, the Three Little Pigs, Goldilocks, and Little Red Riding Hood, to name a few. Superhero movies offer an array of characters who may appear in cartoons doing less than heroic things. History books are replete with larger-than-life characters who provide big targets for cartoonists. An image of Mickey Mouse or Napoleon carries associations that cartoonists can exploit. Paul Noth mashes up both characters (opposite page)—one seen and one implied—to great effect.

Like a cliché setup, fictional and historical characters need no introduction—one glance results in immediate recognition. Even if you haven't plowed through Herman Melville's *Moby-Dick*, a humongous white whale springs to mind. Other sources of classic characters are Greek and Roman mythology—Zeus and Atlas, to name a couple. Sisyphus pops up frequently, perhaps a testament to the frustrations of modern life.

The Bible is a rich source of characters. Think of all the cartoons that feature Adam and Eve, Moses, Saint Peter, Jesus, Satan, and the most frequently depicted character of all, God. The patriarchy may be in jeopardy, but the Supreme Being in the cartoon world is still depicted as an old guy in the clouds with a long, white beard, often behaving no better than the average male.

Then there's a grab-bag of familiar characters, such as the guru on the mountaintop, "end-is-near" guy, and the caveman frescoing his cave, among many others. For cartoonists attracted to dark humor, the medieval image of the Grim Reaper

"I was against Russo-Disneyland from the start."

is their go-to guy. As Joe Dator said in his book *Inked*, "He's fun to draw, and to mess around with, because we know he'll be the one messing around with us eventually."

All of these characters, largely because they are not original but exist independently from the cartoon, have proven to be great source material—so great, in fact, we've thoughtfully included a second appendix of our favorite characters right after the Top 100 cartoon clichés.

META

As mentioned earlier in the chapter, a meta cartoon is a cartoon about cartoons. This self-referencing tactic is especially on display in common cartoon setups and stock cartoon characters that we've discussed. They take the reader behind the curtain to share an inside joke everyone gets. It's like a

film star looking straight at the camera and giving us all a big wink.

One of our favorite meta cartoons is Ellis Rosen's collection of cliché characters hanging out in the backroom of the *New Yorker* magazine, with a stage manager type

"Reaper! You're on in five pages."

giving a heads-up. The cartoon pokes fun at cartoonists who rely on those characters, and the magazines that continue to publish those cartoons. It's fun to see these familiar figures out of their usual contexts, behaving as we might under similar circumstances.

PERSONAL CHARACTERS

Best-selling novelists often develop protagonists who recur in a series of related books. Likewise, movie franchises revolve around a heroic character who defies death to star in the next installment. Similarly, gag cartoonists may develop personal characters—sometimes alter egos—who pop up more than once in their cartoons.

Some of these personal characters occur more frequently than others. For example, in the case of longtime *New Yorker* cartoonist Victoria Roberts, her domestic husband-and-wife duo show up in almost all of her cartoons.

"You know what I want for our twentieth anniversary? A Dumpster."

Another veteran cartoonist, Frank Cotham, based two of his most popular characters on a photograph of his great-great-grandparents, residents of the splendidly named town of Hog Creek, Tennessee. He shared this family photograph with us.

Any resemblance to the couple in his cartoons is purely intentional.

Courtesy of Frank Cotham.

"We're still not seeing a recovery in housing."

"It's off the rack. The guy on the rack doesn't need it anymore."

Kaamran Hafeez developed a recurring character, seemingly out of thin air, whose balding pate and opaque eyeglasses amused him. Family members commented on the resemblance to the artist as this character began showing up regularly in print.

The good-natured cartoonist eventually adopted the character as his Twitter alter ego.

LIFESTYLE SCENARIOS

A few cartoonists, like observational comedians, base their gags on incidents from real life. The settings can be ordinary, such as taking a walk or watching television in the living room. The characters are believable—no alien invaders or Greek gods—just people commenting on the everyday oddities of life, often with unintended irony.

After a decade serving as art director and executive for top New York ad firms, Marisa Acocella developed a keen eye for the fashionistas of Manhattan. In her cartoons, femme fatale vixens carry on withering conversations about vanity, men, and the latest fashions. An inveterate walker, Acocella finds inspiration on the boulevards by spotting glamorous young shoppers and imagining their conversations.

Then, returning to the drawing board, she recreates the glitzy, high-fashion characters and boils down their imaginary conversations into an arch caption.

We've shed some light on the creative process, how cartoonists rely on certain conventions, and how they generate ideas. But what makes the ideas funny? That is the topic of the next chapter.

"Stop complaining. Who isn't broke?"

CHAPTER FIVE

Getting to the Funny

VISUAL INCONGRUITY

In chapter 4, we showed how cartoonists often use cliché setups, stock characters, and other conventions to generate ideas for their cartoons. These conventions can support a comic framework but by themselves aren't funny. It's not enough to show castaways on a desert island, Ahab's unhealthy relationship with Moby-Dick, or gangsters about to dump a guy in a bucket of cement off a pier. And, of course, many cartoonists don't rely on these conventions; they just think of a subject that could lend itself to a humorous twist, whether it's a polar bear, robot, or whatever they happen to see out their window.

How does that comedic twist happen? How do cartoonists bend reality to their will in surprising ways? Consciously or not, many cartoonists apply tried-and-true comedic approaches to create gags on which to base cartoons. We are by no means suggesting that anyone can pick a cliché setup, apply a comedic approach, and produce a uniquely brilliant cartoon. If that were true, you could probably grab a gross of them at Costco, cheap.

We've identified a few approaches that many cartoonists commonly rely on and grouped them under the larger category of Incongruity. Not all cartoons fall neatly into a particular category, and many cartoons have elements common to more than one category. For example, a cartoon may rely on both anachronism and exaggeration. Other cartoons defy categorization—good for them!

Let's start with incongruity.

WHAT IS INCONGRUITY?

When we refer to incongruity in a drawing, we mean the drawing pairs unlike things or presents a scenario with components that don't belong together. The drawing conflicts with reality. What is that kangaroo doing in an airport? Why is a tree talking to a bird? Incongruity is a lens through which cartoonists distort reality. The cartoonist's skill is being able to freely associate things or concepts that are wildly different and discover the common thread that links them. In doing so, the cartoonist reveals what is normally hidden.

Cartoonists think in an untraditional way. Novel ideas spring from the cartoonist's mind because it is not weighed down too heavily by reality. Humor thrives in the cartoonist's skewed vision of the world. Reality, by contrast, is boring, or at least not funny.

We, the readers, must make sense of the incongruity. The more surprising and unexpected the linkage of unlike things, the greater our delight in recognizing that connection. If the connection is obvious, we might find the cartoon less funny or not particularly clever. If the connection is too obscure, we simply won't get it. A great cartoon needs to fall somewhere in between.

Incongruity is an overarching category. Broadly speaking, you can find incongruity in some form in most cartoons. The first step, of course, is to examine the drawing. What sticks out? What seems strange, out of the ordinary? Cartoonists can't afford to be too subtle or the gag misfires. They often exaggerate the contrast between

"Happy?"

incongruous elements in their compositions. Kim Warp does just that in her homage to a literary classic (previous page).

You needn't have read all 135 chapters of *Moby-Dick* to recognize the trophy whale displayed above the mantel. And the incongruity? Instead of, say, a stuffed swordfish, a leviathan dwarfs the tiny figure of peg-legged Captain Ahab relaxing by the fire. Kim Warp cleverly manages to keep the room proportions on the cozy side while somehow implying the whale's full length. She also brilliantly ties the scenario together, thereby resolving the incongruity, with a one-word caption from Ahab's disapproving wife. Unfazed, the good captain serenely puffs on his pipe with smug satisfaction.

More subtle than the visual incongruity is how this imagined scene diverges from the novel's conclusion. Instead of Ahab's tragic end brought about by his hubris, Warp presents an Ahab who has improbably conquered his pale nemesis. Ahab should be dead and the whale alive. In Warp's twist—please, no jokes about the cartoonist's last name—it's the opposite. The humor is unlocked by the wife's acid comment.

Cartoonist Robert Weber provides another example of incongruity, which goes to extremes in pairing unlike things: a sophisticated New York apartment and a fully operational oil pump. The drill rig—known in the business as a "nodding donkey pump"—would look more at home in

"We got a great buy on the apartment, but, unfortunately, it didn't include the mineral rights."

the barren shale basins of West Texas than the leafy Upper East Side of Manhattan. And imagine how the downstairs neighbors must feel!

It's worth noting how Weber cleverly blurs the indoor-outdoor boundaries with a large rug that doubles as bare ground. Nonetheless, how do we make sense of this illogical drawing?

The caption comes to our aid by rationalizing why the apartment owners accepted working drill equipment in their spacious living room. Their one laughable regret is packed into the second half of the caption.

ANACHRONISM

Anachronism refers to a specific type of incongruity cartoon requiring the improbable collision of two historical eras. The drawing can depict today, medieval times, or the primordial past, but something must intrude in the scene from a completely different era. Anachronism cartooning is rich with possibilities: a caveman invents golf, a prim 1800s spinster rides the subway, an Egyptian pharaoh calls his contractor on the phone. Ultimately, no matter which era is chosen, some element must be delightfully out of place, whether in the drawing or the caption.

Here's one of our anachronistic favorites by Julia Suits, set in the modern era. This supermarket looks normal enough. But, uh-oh, barbarians are on the loose, paradoxically, amid the fruits and vegetables.

"We made a bit of a mess in Aisle 2."

Let's take another look at the cartoon, this time as if there were no caption. The drawing alone might need to be clarified. Are these two ruffians from a costume party, a local theater production, or a frat house bash? This is where the cartoonist resolves any ambiguity with a well-phrased caption. No doubt about it, there was some genuine fifth-century pillaging going on.

It is worth noting the cartoon depicts a scene after the main action has occurred and invites us to imagine the "mess in Aisle 2." We don't know exactly what happened there, but given the intruders' frightful appearance, we can be sure it's not pretty. Yet the possibility of a grim outcome is leavened by the almost apologetic comment to the skinny produce kid. After all, they didn't make a big mess, just a bit of a mess.

In this example of anachronism, the past intrudes on the present. The present can also intrude on the past. And the future, in the form of a time traveler, can intrude on the past or present. Often the anachronism is not obvious from the drawing but is instead baked into the caption. For example, a caveman may critique another caveman's cave paintings using the high-flown terms of a pompous art critic. Indeed, without a present-day element, the cartoon probably wouldn't work.

ANTHROPOMORPHISM

Another type of incongruity cartoon incorporates anthropomorphism. You guessed it, cartoons in which cats, dogs, birds, plants—even inanimate objects like telephone poles—behave like humans. Anthropomorphism is a handy tool because it creates a certain distance between the reader and the character, without which the gag would be too obvious, or "on the nose." Putting words in the mouth of a nonhuman, while finding the common element uniting the character and reader, delights us when we recognize ourselves—or someone we know—in the character. Typically, we'll see portrayals of cute domestic pets, because who doesn't love a talking dog? Cartoonist Leo Cullum not only loved talking dogs, but he also didn't mind sticking it to cats either, as shown in his anthropomorphic bar scene.

"It's not enough that we succeed. Cats must also fail."

These dogs simulate high-powered execs in their fancy suits. The dog who's speaking, martini glass in paw, elicits a malevolent expression from his co-conspirator. The drawing asks the fundamental anthropomorphic question: what would a creature—or object, for that matter—say if it could talk? The caption not only answers that question but also hints at a dark desire all dogs likely harbor—to conspire against a certain rival species.

The cartoon also could have worked if the dogs were drawn simply as "normal" talking dogs, say, out for a walk. Instead, by suiting them up, Cullum makes a connection between ruthless businessmen and these two hounds, thereby commenting on the business world. The connection is made more explicit with the well-known quotation, "It's not enough that I succeed, others must fail," attributed to various figures from Genghis Khan to the ultra-competitive co-founder of Oracle, Larry Ellison.

A simpler version of anthropomorphism is Mick Stevens's dog cartoon on the cover of this book.

OUT OF CHARACTER

We expect certain character types to behave in set ways: Santa is jolly, judges are sober-minded, grandmas are kind. When their actions don't conform to type, there is dissonance. If the cartoonist can play *against* our expectations in a clever way, the cartoon will be successful. Cartoons that feature children behaving like adults or, less commonly, adults behaving like children, work on this principle. To cite an example, in the classic cartoon drawn by Carl Rose and captioned by E. B. White that appeared in a 1928 issue of the *New Yorker*, a mother points to the broccoli on her daughter's plate, to which the young girl replies, "I say it's spinach, and I say the hell with it."

We don't imagine that God micromanages his angels, and the Deity certainly wouldn't delegate work on "those commandments" to an underling, but that's the heavenly office scene depicted in Ben Schwartz's cartoon.

God appears less all-powerful than all-overbearing, a boss with nothing better to do than to bug his subordinates about doing God's work. The Almighty and the angel have been reduced to the Earth-bound roles of supervisor and employee. They're

"How we doing on those commandments?"

acting out of character for heavenly beings, but very much in character for office workers. The cartoon is an original, Moses-free take on the Ten Commandments.

SIDE-BY-SIDE CONTRAST

Incongruity can be depicted most dramatically by placing the contrasting elements side by side. One element is familiar and as it should be, and the other element is unfamiliar or out of place. Take for example the cartoon below by Pat Byrnes.

The incongruity exists by adding an alternative to the familiar information kiosk. The contrast is amplified by including a crowd surrounding one and not the other to make a point critical of society: opinions count more than facts.

THE SWITCH

Take a familiar scene and swap out one element to defy expectations. That's an approach we call "the switch." Considered broadly, it applies to a wide array of cartoons, but we begin with a representative example by Shannon Wheeler. The pet almost looks like a shaggy dog—the switch—enough to cause us to look twice. The first sentence of the caption removes any doubt as to the nature of the beast, followed by a pithy punchline. The drawing is simple and effective, but one wonders how he's going to get the animal down those stairs.

Next is a variation on the switch, where the characters' prototypical roles are reversed. Liam Walsh gives a feminist twist to the old damsel-in-distress storyline with

"I'm walking the sloth. See you all in a week"

"Like that?"

an after-the-fact illustration of how it's done. Even though the medieval maiden stands triumphant, wind blowing in her hair, she doesn't want to show up her would-be rescuer, and thus utters a two-word question that answers itself.

EXAGGERATION

Incongruity can be achieved simply by exaggerating one or more elements of a cartoon. An object, a person, in fact almost anything can be drawn much larger or much smaller than it really is. That alone won't make it funny, just unrealistic

or puzzling. The exaggeration must serve a comic purpose. The caption normally explains the disconnect from reality. Let's see how that works with the next cartoon, by Jason Patterson.

Big-box stores are already enormous, so not much exaggeration is needed to show a warehouse that extends across a state line. The high-angle point of view takes in lamps stacked at least four stories tall, blocking out the light, except for the border that separates the lamps from still more lamps in the Iowa section. The sign that we might expect to see on a roadside

incongruously hangs above the home furnishings area, but it makes a kind of sense, considering the exaggerated size of the store. Iowa is a logical choice for a sign that comes out of nowhere, since most non-Iowans probably have trouble locating it on a map of the United States.

While a powerful tool, incongruity is just one method to convey that something's amiss and can only be remedied through a comic lens. As we'll see in the next chapter, where the cartoon includes no incongruity in the drawing, the caption drives the humor.

CHAPTER SIX

Other Pathways to the Funny

CAPTION INCONGRUITY

As we saw in the last chapter, when the drawing contains incongruity, the caption resolves it, following its own peculiar and amusing logic. But what about cartoons with no visual incongruity, where the drawing elements all fit together? For these cartoons, the caption typically *creates* tension between what we expect from a familiar situation and what the cartoon delivers. The incongruity exists not in the drawing but between the drawing and the caption. As with visually incongruous cartoons, we "get" the gag when we resolve that tension. ·

Cartoons with no visual incongruity rely on the drawing to provide a believable setting. For this type of cartoon, the focus is on the caption, less so on the drawing.

Unlike visually incongruous cartoons, which sometimes are caption-less, these cartoons always have captions.

Think of the drawing as the setup of a joke and the caption as the punchline. "A man walks into a bar" is a classic opening line used by generations of standup comedians. We can picture the scene: the bar's interior, rows of liquor bottles, a customer or two, and of course, the indispensable bartender. So far, nothing to laugh at or to figure out. Finally, someone—the man, bartender, customer—says something. A comedian will act out the verbal exchange that concludes with the punchline. We laugh because the punchline is so unexpected—even at odds with the verbal exchange. Similarly, a cartoon's drawing sets our expectations, and the caption typically defies them. The caption does the heavy comedic lifting.

That's not to say the drawing in these cartoons is unimportant. It must convey the scene clearly so as not to frustrate the reader. The drawing also imparts the mood, from dark to delightful, silly to strange. And certain talented cartoonists—many of whom we highlight later in the book—have styles that captivate us at first glimpse.

Jason Adam Katzenstein's true-to-life illustration style takes us between rounds in a boxing match. The square-jawed pugilist awaits advice from his corner man. "Watch out for his right hook" or "Careful of his left uppercut" are turns of phrase every boxer has heard, but the cartoonist's caption concludes with a jab at the boxer himself.

Cartoons that present realistic scenarios as a pathway to humor have been a mainstay of cartoonists for generations, and it's easy to see why: the cartoonist can choose from a range of plausible situations to set up the tension between the drawing and the caption. Here below are a few broad categories.

EVERYDAY SITUATIONS

At its core, the category of everyday situations is about the routine of work, school, holidays, and, especially, home sweet home.

"Watch out for his being better at boxing than you."

We recognize this world—it's about us. Our cartoonists reflect this world and our evolving culture with unexpected insights into life's minor ironies and mini-dramas.

Sometimes the settings are little more than backdrops—a cartoon, say, depicting a snippet of conversation between friends in a café or a kitchen—but more often the setting contributes to the gag. Familiar, realistic settings create specific expectations in the reader's mind as to how the characters will react, but we also know that the cartoonist will surprise us by having someone say something out of the ordinary. The trick for the cartoonist is to confound our expectations while coming up with something completely original.

What could be more ordinary than seeing someone walking along and talking on their cell phone? We often overhear one side of these conversations and note how mundane they sound. Aware of this phenomenon, cartoonist Harry Bliss presents an unremarkable scene while slyly unleashing a caption that startles our sensibilities. The drawing: ordinary. The caption: extraordinary. Warning: do not try this gag in real life!

It's also worth noting how once common cartoon situations have been replaced by others, reflecting societal changes. For example, two businessmen downing drinks in a bar was an old cartoon setting standby, now fading with time. Conversely, as we discuss in chapter 10, the characters in contemporary cartoons increasingly

"Honey, let me call you back—I'm bored."

represent our diverse social, racial, and ethnic backgrounds.

Cartoons about everyday situations is such a broad category that it merits breaking down. We begin with cartoons where the tension is muted.

GENERIC SETTINGS

Certain cartoons are of the "talking head" variety. We don't mean that as a criticism; it's just that they typically depict one person commenting to someone else. The setting is not integral to the gag.

With this type of cartoon, the gag likely arrives fully formed in the cartoonist's mind. Having the caption in hand, the cartoonist gives life to the cartoon by producing a credible setting. Several options will come to mind, all serviceable. The gag might work just as well in a variety of everyday settings—in a home, on the street, or in a backyard—although not in extraordinary settings, such as a desert, a jungle, or the moon.

The drawing itself tends not to be overtly humorous. It serves as a background and should not call undue attention to itself. The relative blandness of the setting functions to speed up the transfer of the reader's attention to the caption.

A master of this genre was William Hamilton. Hundreds of his cartoons gently satirizing the upper crust ran in the *New Yorker*. He knew East Coast elitists well, having graduated from Phillips Academy and Yale. His largely interchangeable characters were often foolish and self-absorbed, spouting unintentionally ironic remarks to their social equals while keeping a firm grip on a cocktail glass. Hamilton created a world just slightly off-center from the one he observed, and accomplished that with an instantly recognizable artistic style. As his drawings included no incongruity, satirical observation formed the pathway for his humor. Hamilton was a social critic, standing on the periphery of the high society he critiqued.

The characters in this cartoon are the usual suspects: old, white men in business suits boozing and smoking. But what is the setting? Perhaps a private men's club or someone's apartment on Manhattan's Upper East Side, but aside from the barest suggestion of a couple of chairs, the cartoonist gives us no clue. The setting has all but disappeared, leaving a cluster of similar-minded businessmen to celebrate

"This just might be the greatest period of privatization since feudalism."

their good fortune. It's as though the suits themselves create the setting, crowding out any trappings of an interior.

So where is the tension between the almost nonexistent setting and the caption? It's subtle when the characters essentially are the setting, but it exists in that we expect these blue-blood executives to be more discreet in celebrating the reaping of their financial rewards. Instead, we witness their full-throated embrace of unabashed greed in cosseted privacy.

Another cartoonist whose settings are at times secondary to the gag is Victoria Roberts. Her little domestic vignettes often take place in a living room. The pathway to the humor is the quirky but pithy observation. The settings may be unremarkable, but the theatrically costumed woman who frequently appears in her work is not (see below).

On the next page, we have one more example from cartoonist Peter Vey, a prolific producer of offbeat humor. Does it matter where this conversation takes place? It does not. These gents could just as well be inside the bar they are walking past. The gag is barely tied to the artwork. In fact, the caption could be a line spoken by a standup comedian.

"Don't worry, Howard. The big questions are multiple choice."

"As part of new security measures, Doris has locked me out of the house."

Note how the speaker's hand in his pocket suggests a casualness at odds with his statement. His mouth is barely open, and his glasses hide any emotion he might otherwise betray. As with many Vey cartoons, the wildly unexpected comment is delivered deadpan. The caption works its magic, economically balancing the setup and punchline. For dry, wry humor, he's one of the best.

Specific Settings

More often, cartoons about everyday situations are tied to specific settings. The Dator cartoon about having children is logically set in the bedroom. In the same vein, a work-related cartoon will be set in an office. In these cartoons, the setting serves a function, like the staging in a play, by grounding the characters in a particular environment and providing information about the relationships between the characters.

Teresa Burns Parkhurst gives us the office meeting setup. A certain decorum is expected under these circumstances. If unavoidably delayed, one offers an apology and a valid—if sometimes fictional—reason for being late. Parkhurst's latecomer defies convention, and our expectations, by being completely honest.

"Sorry I'm late. I got caught up at home being happy."

The caption is what we might expect right up to the last two words, springing the surprise ending. There's truth in the humor—we'd rather be home. Of course, you can't say that in real life, so cartoons provide the outlet.

SPECIAL AND CLICHÉ SITUATIONS

Cartoonists also take aim at special situations, often stress-producing, that demand a particular setting. A wedding, funeral, hospital stay, and job interview, to name a few, are rich sources for cartoon humor.

Because these situations dictate a specific environment—think funeral—the universe of potential gags narrows. At the same time, our associations with special situations are stronger than with everyday situations. That makes playing on our expectations easier and increases the tension between drawing and caption.

Anyone familiar with the work of veteran cartoonist Frank Cotham wouldn't be surprised to learn that he has a pessimistic outlook on life. A doctor delivering a crushing diagnosis to a patient, medieval serfs toiling in mud, duelists at dawn—all qualify as subjects of mirth for Cotham. His cartoons always have a specific atmosphere that is crucial to his cartoons. His captions are jarringly at odds with the somber scenes. Consider the specimen below.

Given the scene, we expect grim news for the patient or perhaps words of medical wisdom from the senior physician. And indeed, the caption begins with what we assume will be an appropriate observation, but concludes with an unexpected

"This patient has a rare form of medical insurance."

twist. The cartoon works as satire because it highlights a truth: medical care follows medical insurance. Everyone absorbs this wisdom soberly, except, that is, for the skeptical patient.

Take a moment to study this drawing. Despite the ceiling lights and large wall lamp, the scene looks depressingly dark. Is this hospital room fitted inside a cave? The shadows are inky, and the curtain, while illuminated to highlight the figures standing before it, appears funereal. Note also how the light reflects on certain objects, such as the bed rail and the patient chart. One does not just look at a Frank Cotham cartoon; one descends into it.

Leo Cullum approached his subject, an emergency mid-flight announcement, by twisting the usual phrase in an unexpected way. The result? A great satirical cartoon about the airline industry, a subject he knew well; he was a commercial airline pilot as well as a brilliant cartoonist.

Of course, to get the gag, a reader needs to know that in recent decades airlines have entered and exited bankruptcy proceedings

"Ladies and gentlemen, is there a bankruptcy attorney on board?"

as easily as a jet through a cloud bank. Passengers should still buckle up. It could be a bumpy ride.

The cartoon cliché is so durable that it can serve as the setting for cartoons with or without incongruity in the drawing. We know the setups and characters: a lawyer arguing to a jury, an executive pointing to a sales chart, or a mutineer walking the plank. Because we have such strong associations with characters in cartoon cliché situations, the cartoonist may strive to come up with a caption that is particularly dissonant. As

with special situation cartoons, the humor possibilities are somewhat limited by the cliché setup. But narrowing the field of humor can also help the cartoonist focus on the best gags.

Let's eavesdrop on a happy occasion —a wedding. Cartoonists lampoon vows at the altar so frequently that it's become a cherished cliché. We have positive associations joining two soulmates, as well as respect for the occasion's solemnity. So, of course, cartoonists subvert this expectation. The great Jack Ziegler, not known

"First marriage?"

for respecting traditions, drops a comic bomb.

Smiles are all around. Even the goofy groom looks pleased. He's just making small talk as he and his bride begin their life journey together. Oh, yes—the bride. Her face seems frozen. She may be asking herself, "Who is this guy I just said 'I do'

to?" His flippant two-word inquiry is so monstrously inappropriate that it's funny . . . very funny.

All of these cartoons rely on a cleverly worded caption to birth the humor. In the next chapter, we'll consider how great captions create great cartoons—and how some cartoons go bare.

CHAPTER SEVEN

Say What?

CAPTIONS AND CAPTIONLESS

As discussed in previous chapters, when the drawing includes incongruous elements, the caption resolves, more or less, the drawing's discordant parts. When the drawing does not include incongruity, the caption may *create* incongruity by being at odds with the drawing. We presented examples of both situations in various settings. Now we'll examine more closely how words and drawings together produce humor, how the wording of the caption is critical to the gag, and when a drawing alone can be a great cartoon.

CARTOONS WITH CAPTIONS
CAPTION GUIDELINE #1: KEEP IT SHORT.

Most people look at the drawing first, then the caption . . . and probably glance again

"Phil!"

at the drawing. For that reason, a good caption should communicate with the drawing, as if there's a dialogue between them. That's literally the case in this "desert crawler" cartoon by Julia Suits.

The caption and the drawing are in perfect harmony. And the one-word caption perfectly illustrates our first caption guideline.

Try to stay within a dozen words; otherwise, the average reader will skip it. Though one simple sentence or phrase works best, combining two sentences or phrases can achieve a more complex effect. Using an example from the previous chapter, Leo Cullum uses a period between two short sentences to create a sense of malice: "It's not enough that we succeed. Cats must also fail." A well-placed em-dash in Harry Bliss's cartoon gives comic timing to the speaker's insulting request, "Honey, let me call you back—I'm bored."

CAPTION GUIDELINE #2: PUT THE FUNNY AT THE END.

Effective captions compel the reader to look at the drawing in a new light. An astute observer of relationships, William Haefeli shows a couple in a well-appointed, somewhat cluttered dwelling. He's talking to her; she's doing something else—the tension appears low. Moving

"I'm ready to go whenever you're through fussing with tablescapes."

on to Haefeli's arch caption, the phrase "fussing with tablescapes" causes us to reexamine the drawing more closely. Now the reader can't miss the obsessive over-decorating of every flat surface. We also understand the motive behind the man's sarcastic exasperation. Borrowed from the event planning world, "fussing with tables-capes" gets our attention. And where does Haefeli put this evocative phrase? At the end.

CAPTION GUIDELINE #3: A TWO-PART CAPTION CREATES EXPECTATIONS AND THEN DASHES THEM.

Captions can contain two opposing ideas. The fulcrum for these ideas is often a comma separating two phrases. In terms of comedic function, the first phrase sets up the gag, and the second unleashes the punchline. A drawing showing one person talking to another best serves this type of caption.

"You can afford to retire at 65, but you'll need to die at 70."

Co-author Phil Witte gives hope in one phrase, then takes it away with the second. This cartoon is a variation of the "good news/bad news" gag, where the caption creates expectations and then defies them. If the order of the two phrases were flipped, the meaning would be the same, but it wouldn't be funny. So, save the surprise for the end.

The "good news/bad news" gag works best if the bad news far outweighs the good news.

CAPTION GUIDELINE #4: USE UNUSUAL OR FUNNY-SOUNDING WORDS.

Captions can be worded in many ways to express the same idea, but choosing the word that best conveys the humor is critical. Consider Sam Gross's wonderfully absurd take on the desert crawler cartoon below.

It's an example of incongruity writ large, "explained" by the caption. The two-part construction adheres to the rule that the surprising element lands at the end. But what drives the humor is the caption's final word, "krill." That choice of that word illustrates this guideline.

Words that are specific and unusual can light up a caption. "Plankton" could work in the caption, but not as well as "krill," a delightfully odd word. "Krill" also sounds funnier. Comedians have known since the vaudeville days that words with the letter "k" are funny. "Plankton" has a "k," but "krill" trumps "plankton."

"First, let's concentrate on water. Then we'll worry about krill."

CAPTION GUIDELINE #5: TWIST A COMMON TURN OF PHRASE.

Evocative turns of phrases, metaphors, and other linguistic techniques can add interest to an otherwise straightforward narrative, but when overused, they become tiresome and practically meaningless. The business world in particular indulges in clichés that are somehow meant to inspire.

J. C. Duffy slices and dices a couple of moldy metaphors to assemble a word salad

"It's come to my attention that you've been pushing the box and thinking outside the envelope, Jenson."

devoid of sense. The boss, in his mind at least, has made himself clear.

Cartoons relying on this technique are not common, but done well they can startle a reader by rendering something new from old material.

CAPTION GUIDELINE #6: UNDERSTATE REACTIONS.

When a situation calls for a more emphatic response, but a character instead utters a low-key remark, a conflict arises between our expectation and the caption. Where there's conflict, the possibility for humor exists. We rely on Peter Vey for an example.

This suburban scene looks normal—nothing about the characters suggests anything is amiss—until one peeks inside the house and the absurdity of the situation is revealed. The caption does not resolve the incongruity; rather, it creates tension between the drawing and the characters'

"Don't forget to call the Fire Department."

reactions. This cartoon also offers another angle to writing funny captions.

Granted, exaggerated responses to everyday experiences can create comic possibilities. In both cases, someone is not behaving normally, or at least not how we expect them to react. We prefer the understated response. As we discussed in the "Types of Humor" chapter, understatement pairs well with dry humor.

CAPTION GUIDELINE #7: DON'T OVEREXPLAIN.

Great cartoonists respect the reader. They know that piecing together the disparate components of a cartoon is part of the pleasure. This cartoon by Christopher Weyant, who, incidentally, is also a political cartoonist and children's book illustrator, lets the reader fill in the gap.

"Mistakes were made."

A caption should reveal the gag, not explain it. Leave something to the reader's imagination, so the reader can figure out how the caption and drawing work together. In Weyant's cartoon, the man behind the podium offers none, but we can surmise the preceding events, who the speaker is, and who the surviving audience member is. Note also how using the passive voice, suggesting that fault lies elsewhere, boosts the humor.

CAPTION GUIDELINE #8: CLEVER WORD ARRANGEMENT PUNCHES UP THE PUNCH LINE.

Captions can also rely on wordplay to generate humor. We're not referring to the common pun, which can be occasionally amusing but seldom warrants a drawing. In our view, unusual word arrangements rank higher on the humor scale. Take Kim Warp's office cartoon. Warp's caption invites a reread to confirm the deceptive "work from work" phrasing. The wording is precise and even sounds like a logical request.

"We were hoping that you could work from work today."

It offers a lesson to aspiring cartoonists.

Word arrangement generally factors into a cartoon's success. The caption should have a natural rhythm that flows off the tongue if spoken aloud.

In each of these examples, a character says something inappropriate or unexpected under the circumstances. Even if the statement is illogical, it must comment on or at least relate to the situation depicted for the cartoon to have any chance of landing a laugh. But if the character is silent, what then? Read on . . .

CARTOONS WITH WORDS IN THE DRAWING

Cartoonists feel no restriction about where to add words to their cartoons. They'll most commonly add a sentence or two underneath the drawing, which we've defined as a caption. But that's only one convention. Cartoonists also place words into signs, title boxes, and speech/thought balloons. And because those words are integral to the drawing, we engage with them differently than with a caption. Why? Because of the way we read cartoons. Unlike a caption, we read the various signs, boxes, and balloons *before* we absorb the drawing.

Take a look at Mick Stevens's somber cartoon of dystopian desolation. We can't help but read the prominent title box first, placed top center by the artist. Then we take in the drawing's bleak scene. In a reversal of captioned cartoons, the title box text "Life Without Mozart" is the setup, and the drawing is the "punchline."

Labels in a cartoon must do more than simply identify an object; they must be integrated into the gag. A prime example is a storefront sign theme by John Jonik on the next page.

LIFE WITHOUT MOZART

The gag follows two of our guidelines for captioned cartoons: it's a twist on a common expression, and the funny part, unspoken, lands at the end.

Like all artists, cartoonists are inveterate rulebreakers. No sooner do we declare a dozen or so words the limit for a caption than someone, Joe Dator, in this case, begs to differ. He shatters the world record for caption length at 103 words. The "caption" is enclosed within a cloud-shaped balloon, indicating thoughts, not spoken words. Here, the thought balloon has inflated so large that it blocks out most of the drawing.

So much for keeping it brief. Not a caption per se but a stream-of-conscious outpouring of observations and confessions of desire by a nineteenth-century maiden on a modern-day subway car. The gag is based on anachronism, but the incongruity of someone seemingly dropping from the long-ago past into the present isn't resolved by the thought balloon. Instead, the woman's thoughts, phrased in the delicate prose of a romance novel of a bygone age, become increasingly absurd. Her attraction to the schlub sitting across from her is not explained, making her—and perhaps the Austenesque novel in which such a character could exist—ridiculous.

CARTOONS WITHOUT WORDS

The difficulty of producing a successful cartoon increases enormously when the cartoonist doesn't rely on a caption, sign, speech balloon, or words of any kind. Forget about wordplay, funny words, and clever turns of phrases to elicit a laugh. Because the powerful tool of words isn't employed, there is no punchline. Without the guidance of a caption, one must search for, sort out, and resolve the disparate elements. The humor lies in the art. Any incongruity in the drawing cannot be resolved except through the drawing itself.

John O'Brien is another cartoonist-illustrator who stands out for his excellence within this challenging tradition. He creates miniature worlds that look like timeless etchings. What at first glance may appear bewildering reveals itself to be a vividly imagined world.

O'Brien turns the familiar warning sign for a deer crossing into a flip card of animation that can only be experienced from the window of a passing car. As viewers, we cannot appreciate the movement but can imagine what the car's passengers see. Both in execution and design, a brilliant cartoon.

Like the game charades, a cartoon in this category must present clues without the benefit of language. In this example, Liana Finck finds inspiration in Picasso by depicting well-known literary figures as silhouettes. Incongruities abound as we take in the spear-wielding Spaniard astride a chair next to a modern door. As we follow Don Quixote's upward gaze, we recognize the literary sendup in the windmilling fan. True to his character, the unperturbable Sancho continues to doze.

Of the current generation of cartoonists following this path, few can compete with Seth Fleishman for originality and striking artwork.

There are other cartoons about vampires casting no reflection in mirrors, but setting Dracula in a canoe on a glassy lake is truly inspired. In the words of Bob Mankoff, "It's just a joy to look at these little complications of frames put together in this elegant way. They're all just little jewels."

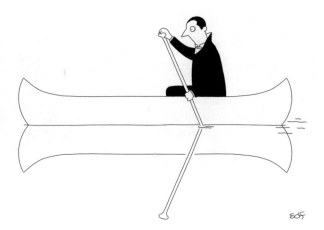

CHAPTER EIGHT

Drawing Funny

ILLUSTRATION STYLES

The first thing we consider when we come across a cartoon? The drawing, of course. Not only does it depict a scene and present a situation with comic possibilities, but it also creates a mood and affects our emotions. This is especially true when the cartoonist has a unique and recognizable style that contributes to and is well-suited to the cartoonist's humor. When the art and the gag work together, a great cartoon emerges.

DEVELOPING A STYLE

For some cartoonists, their artistic style is simply a mature version of how they drew as children. Along the way, they may have learned perspective drawing, how to emphasize the critical elements of the cartoon, and other artistic skills, but their basic style can be traced to their youthful efforts.

For some of the finest cartoonists, however, the process was long and tortuous. Jack Ziegler, one of the best cartoonists of his generation, recalled, "It wasn't until about my five-thousandth drawing that I began to like what I was seeing, but that didn't happen for another ten years." In his unpublished memoir, Ziegler recalled how early in his career he drew in an overly realistic style:

> [P]eople with real faces, clothing that was creased with wrinkles, shoes that looked like cordovans with handsome, well-tied laces, soles and heels a separate entity from the upper body of the shoe, with expertly crafted wrinkles in the leather. Always the wrinkles. I'd gone overboard on the wrinkles. Not to mention the faces, where

I'd been delineating manly jawlines that traveled all the way from chin to earlobe.

Brian McConnachie, on the staff of the *National Lampoon*, told him that his artwork was "too formal" and that his cartoons "have no life to them." He offered this advice: "If the style were freer, the joke would come through. Now it looks forced. You have to relax. . . . It's always better when you do them just for yourself, which is why roughs are usually better than the finished product."

Ziegler took the advice and began producing cartoons in a simplified style.

I started to see the difference this made in my work and almost immediately began to experience a bit of enjoyment in what I was doing. . . . I had recently realized that my favorite cartoons were always ones conjured up from the silliest, dumbest situations possible. In order to pull these off, I saw that my drawings had to be of a simplicity that would match the idiocy I was seeking. . . . Soon all of my well-executed eyes had devolved into mere dots. Full heads of hair were now just a couple of lines. And jawlines? Forget about it.

Ziegler continued:

Poor old, nearly blind James Thurber had done some of the funniest cartoons in the *New Yorker*'s early days precisely because he couldn't see well enough to draw properly, and this had made all the difference. The wackier the idea, the simpler the drawing needed to be for its genuine mirth to shine through.

Ziegler's journey to artistic discovery may give hope to cartoonists struggling to create a unique and pleasing style. Ziegler had the good fortune to have an astute editor critique his work. He realized that the realism of his drawing weighed down his absurd sense of humor. Once Ziegler corrected the mismatch, everything clicked into place. He became a different and far better cartoonist.

Great cartoonists create a unique world with art that is instantly recognizable. Their cartoons are like rooms in their mind set down on paper, an imagined reality. A reader enters a George Booth cartoon, for example, and stands in the living room like an eavesdropper.

RANGE OF STYLES FROM SPARE TO LUSH

SPARE STYLE

In the broadest sense, we've chosen to categorize cartoon styles as either spare or lush. The spare style cartoon relies on an unvarying line thickness with little or no shading or gray tones and only enough detail to convey the scene. Cartoonists who favor this approach have no fear of white space. As Ziegler noted, James Thurber, known as much for his humor writing as for his cartooning, is a prime example of this style. This classic Thurber cartoon from a 1932 issue of the *New Yorker* epitomizes a simplicity that approaches abstraction. Note, for example, how the arms of the couple are merely suggested.

"All right, have it your way—you heard a seal bark!"

Courtesy of Michael Maslin.

"Hold on, this is the stick—I asked for the ball."

A similarly pared-down style can be seen in the cartoons of many artists in this book, including Mick Stevens, Bruce Eric Kaplan, Amy Hwang, and David Sipress, as well as Liza Donnelly, Jean Jacques Sempé, P. S. Mueller, Bob Eckstein, and Mort Gerberg.

Michael Maslin's work pays homage to Thurber's style, an influence he has acknowledged. In Maslin's cartoon, above, of a botched fetching, he uses a simple, uniform-width line to tell the story.

There's a gentleness to these simply drawn cartoons with their vague, wandering lines. The settings are basic but unambiguously real. The characters connect on a human level, or in the case of the Maslin cartoon, a human-to-canine level. The humor is whimsical.

Barbara Smaller's cartoons exemplify the spare style. The execution is sketchy, even a bit vague (see opposite page). Shadows are evoked on the ceiling and walls with sharp, little pen strokes. And what are those little, curved marks on the floor?

As with Maslin's cartoons, line thickness doesn't vary. Although the style is simple, Smaller draws fully furnished rooms occupied by characters drawn from head to toe, never cropped. They often appear nonplussed in the face of domestic conflict.

"The thing is, I've grown and you haven't."

A spare style can also be powerful. For a direct, bold line style, no one comes close to Charles Barsotti. Relatable kings and cute puppies, often on a psychologist's couch, are his go-to characters. A telephone on a stool is a typical prop. His technique is simplicity itself, but perfecting that elegant style requires great skill.

Barsotti's characters may be as emotionally distressed as Roz Chast's New Yorkers, but they're far more loveable. They appear to exist in a hybrid fairy-tale world, where medieval monarchs confront modern concerns. We're not as emotionally affected by these make-believe characters, allowing us to laugh at them without judgment.

"You're why I have the moat, Mother."

LUSH STYLE

A lush style—exuberant, grand, sophisticated, and ornate—was dominant in the mid-twentieth century, when magazine cartoons were produced in large formats. It was common to find a full-page cartoon in bold color by Erich Sokol in *Playboy* or richly inked by Peter Arno in the *New Yorker*. These cartoonists were virtuosos in their field.

None of the artists in this deeply realized style reached the success of Charles Addams, whose fame rests not only on his magazine cartoons but also on the ghoulish family of characters who became familiar to TV viewers from the show *The Addams Family* (1964–1966). Two motion pictures also featured Addams' characters and delighted audiences with the same macabre humor of Addams' cartoons.

Addams' eccentric world combined horror house thrills with the graphic edginess of Grand Guignol theater. His melodramatic graphic style bears witness to

© 1940 Charles Addams, Renewed 1985. With permission from the Tee and Charles Addams Foundation.

the bizarre. In his Christmas-gone-wrong cartoon, the high angle, rich detail, and sharp shadows lend a sense of drama to this unfolding of an unfortunate event. The only white in this inky illustration appears as snow. Every element occupies three-dimensional space. Not a mere drawing—this is a black and white composition fit for a museum.

A worthy heir to this exuberant style was Lee Lorenz. In addition to being a prolific cartoonist, he served as the cartoon editor at the *New Yorker* for twenty-five years, preceding Mankoff. His brushwork was dramatic, sweeping, and seemingly effortless.

Before we read the caption, the art conveys a joyous mood and a sense of exuberance. We gleefully enter this world of excess and are primed for a gag that relies on exaggeration. An over-the-top style is appropriate, given that the target of the humor is the "problems" of the rich.

"Forgive the mess. Warren just put everything into cash."

The staircase is realistically convincing, even though the lines are broken, missing, or askew. The oval portraits lining the wall would be unrecognizable in isolation, but easily understood in context. Few cartoonists could draw a crystal chandelier with such casual elegance. And how to illustrate mountains of paper money? Lorenz found a way. The art is so extraordinary that it elevates the cartoon's gag to greater comedic heights.

Robert Weber combined a casual graphic style that conveyed a sense of urbane sophistication while mildly mocking the lifestyles he depicted.

The image looks as messy as real life. Note that the background elements, such as the bookcase full of books, are mere scribbles. Yet its very casualness makes it inviting and fun.

William Haefeli is another cartoonist whose cartoons merit close inspection. He

"Daddy, what collar is a novelist, white or blue?"

"And this is what the tattoo you've chosen will look like in thirty years."

favors compact scenes packed with extraordinary detail. His tattoo parlor scenario is a fine example.

Haefeli's artistic virtuosity multiplies the cartoon's impact. The illusion of textures alone is a study in graphic art. Haefeli imbues the man's jeans and desk surface with an almost tactile quality. Our eyes travel from the hipster's inked skin to the tattoo designs on the computer and in frames on the walls. He achieves this astonishing range of tonal effects with pencils and a black marker, never with ink washes. The resulting textures and shades of gray-to-black give the image a vibrancy that few cartoonists can hope to achieve.

In contrast to the room's realism, his characters' faces appear flattened, like paper cutouts, with simple, sharp noses, enormous ears lacking any detail, minimal eyes, and zero chin. Yet there is no mistaking how closely these characters interact with each other, largely due to their engaged postures. By combining verisimilitude and caricature, Haefeli creates an eccentric world that intrigues us.

This tradition also appears, to a varying degree, in the cartoons of Marisa Acocella, Leo Cullum, Kaamran Hafeez, Ellis Rosen, and Brooke Bourgeois, among others. But the artistic virtuoso, once prized among magazine editors, has become rare in recent years. As Bob Mankoff once put it, "It's the think, not the ink." But Mankoff has since reconsidered. "One of the things that's happened with cartooning is that the pendulum has swung too far to people who don't have enough artistic talent."

Many cartoonists don't fall squarely into the spare or lush tradition; they fall somewhere in between. Some cartoonists may rely on a uniform line but create complex compositions. George Price comes to mind. Others, like Roz Chast, make liberal use of gray tones but keep the scenes unadorned to focus attention on the gag.

Characterizing illustration styles as either more spare or more lush is just one approach to gaining a deeper understanding of the artwork. Styles are as individualistic as the cartoonists associated with them. That's part of their charm. "One of the greatest, most wonderful things about cartooning," said Chast, "is that it's so much up to the person doing it and how they want to do it. There's no one way."

UNUSUAL STYLES

A few cartoonists have unusual styles that stand out. No one other than Mankoff creates cartoons in the pointillist style. Edward Koren's characters are composed of tiny scratch marks with bird-like beaks. Lars Kenseth has described his oddly shaped characters as "capsule people." His eccentric style may alienate some, but it pairs well with his quirky humor. Can Edward Steed draw well? It doesn't matter. His images unapologetically convey a brutal world peopled by perverse and horrible characters—but funny because they serve the gag.

Highly personal styles offer an entry into the cartoonist's mind. "I really like some of the newer people who are drawing naive stuff," said veteran cartoonist Mick Stevens. "I think it's not because they can't draw. It's because they're trying to tear it down to the basics. I'm charmed by some of that, like Liana Finck's work. It's just like you're in her brain. It's her own very personal world and she's sharing it."

Drew Dernavich is known for cartoons that resemble woodcuts. He doesn't draw the images; he engraves them on white scratchboard. First, he drops blobs of ink on the areas that he wants to work on; then, after it dries, he carves away the ink to reveal the white surface underneath. The result (see opposite page) is a formal, rather cold-looking tableau that intrigues more than invites the reader.

Before turning to cartooning, Dernavich engraved pictures onto gravestones, a unique path to becoming a professional cartoonist.

For a description of the many tools cartoonists use—pens, pencils, paper, inks, brushes, erasers, charcoal, watercolors, grease crayons, and markers—check out Jane Mattimoe's blog, *A Fine Case for Pencils*, at afinecaseforpencils.com.

"Any of these guys look like the Peeping Tom?"

GOING DIGITAL

The tool that many cartoonists now swear by can't be found in art supply stores: a digital drawing tablet. The advantages over traditional tools are obvious. Drawing on a tablet takes less time because lines can be deleted, redrawn, or moved in seconds; and digital tablets can be taken anywhere. Not long ago, the mechanically straight and uniform lines and overall coldness of the image made it easy to detect which cartoons were created on a tablet. The technology has since evolved, allowing for greater depth and tone, so that now the distinctions are less apparent.

Speed and ease of use have converted many ink-stained cartoonists to go digital; however, others still prefer the tactile experience of pen and brush on paper. Whether using a tablet or a pen, most cartoonists rely on Photoshop or another app to clean up stray marks before emailing jpegs or pdfs of their cartoons to editors.

IS IT ART?

Most people don't think of cartoons in the same way that they think of a painting in a museum or even grandma's watercolors. But it takes skill—artistic skill—to draw an effective cartoon. So is it art, at least in the

same way that book illustrations, advertising images, movie posters, and Campbell soup cans are art?

Since everyone has an opinion about art, one way to resolve this issue is to put it to a vote. Phil Witte, cartoonist, and co-author of this book, imagines a populist approach to aesthetics that museums may wish to consider.

Harry Bliss, who studied at the Pennsylvania Academy of Fine Arts, has an emphatic answer with respect to his own work: "Cartooning for me is my art. I take it very seriously. It's highbrow, it's Daumier. . . . Being a great cartoonist is the tops." Bliss takes enormous care in his drawing. At the same time, he told us, "If you have a clever idea, I can overlook shoddy drawing very easily." Roz Chast, a graduate of the Rhode Island School of Design (RISD) who has developed a highly personal artistic vocabulary, has a similar view: "I'm not a critic of draftsmanship because in many ways, I don't really care that much about it as long as it serves the joke well." Both stress the interplay between the drawing and the gag.

Bliss, who started out as a book cover illustrator and who has drawn more than twenty covers of the *New Yorker*, makes the point that good cartoonists are rarer than good illustrators because cartooning requires the additional ability to generate humorous ideas: "I can appreciate a good picture—you know, nicely drawn and a nice composition—but there are a lot of people who can do that . . . . But there aren't a lot of people whose brains work in a specific way where they can comment in a unique way about how they see the world."

Whether or not cartoons qualify as art, many cartoonists are artists who have applied their skills to create cartoons. Quite a number have received degrees from art schools. John O'Brien studied at the Philadelphia College of Art, Peter Vey at the School of Visual Arts in New York, and Lee Lorenz, Paul Karasik, Peter Kuper, and Edward Koren attended the Pratt Institute. In fact, Lorenz studied with renowned artist Philip Guston, whose later work received criticism for resembling crudely drawn cartoons.

A few cartoonists have minimized the value of their training. Frank Cotham confided to us, "I got a bachelor of fine arts degree from the University of Memphis, which has been absolutely useless." Roz Chast believed that RISD respected only "serious" art, and Liana Finck felt her time at Cooper Union actually stifled her creative instincts.

Several artists began working in the fine arts before migrating to cartooning. David Sipress, for example, wanted to be a cartoonist since elementary school, but he didn't work full-time as a cartoonist until age fifty, when he gave up his twenty-year career as a sculptor.

Saul Steinberg combined a career as artist and illustrator with great success in each area. He's best known for a *New Yorker* cover—much imitated by others—that depicted a "map" of the world from a Manhattanite's point of view that basically ends at the Hudson River. But decades before that cover appeared, New York's Museum of Modern Art exhibited his work. Dozens of museums include his drawings in their permanent collections. Steinberg was a singular talent whose creations were equal parts art, humor, and intellect. His pen and ink drawings, whether simple or Baroque, contain meaning that is best expressed—perhaps can only be expressed—in art.

So where does that leave us? Isn't art what passes as art?

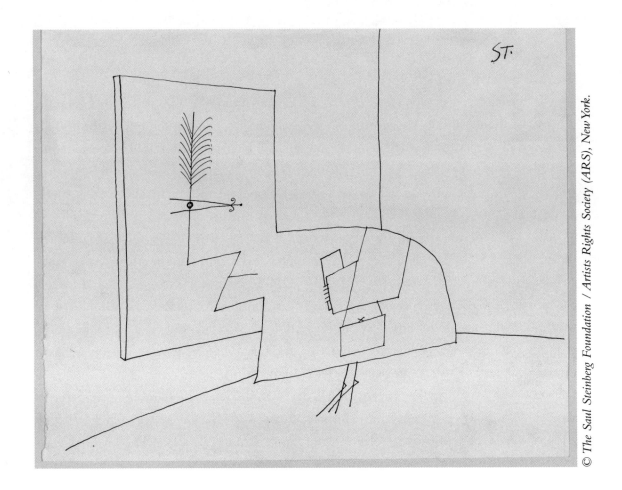

Now we're about to enter the mind of
the cartoonist. Ready?

CHAPTER NINE

Twisted

THE PSYCHE OF THE CARTOONIST

The cartoonist's mind works differently. As detached observers, they must recognize and distill complex situations into a single image. Their inspiration can come from a turn of phrase, a moment on the street, or a doodle coaxed into a drawing. The extraordinary range of approaches to the art form varies with the personalities of the artists. Their upbringing, temperament, and individual quirks inform the humor. As Peter Vey told us, not entirely seriously, the compulsion to create "is like having a mental illness that I work out in cartoons."

We've identified a few of our favorite cartoonists whose body of work shows a consistent outlook that offers a peek into their psyches. We present them in three groups:

Off-Kilter: Those artists whose idiosyncrasies are a wellspring of ideas and characters.

Everyday Celebrants: Keen social observers who skewer our human foibles.

The Outrageous Ones: Boundary-crossing adventurers who dare to create impossible, perplexing, and even disturbing scenarios.

OFF-KILTER

THE NEUROTIC: ROZ CHAST

If there's one cartoonist that readers of the *New Yorker* might know, it's likely to be Roz Chast. For decades, almost every issue of the magazine has included one of her cartoons. The characters are often anxious urbanites or dopey middle-aged people failing to find meaning in life, simply because they don't look very hard.

Chast has written and spoken extensively about her childhood, and thus a direct line can be drawn from her anxious upbringing to her neurotic cartoon characters. In her world, there is always something to worry about, no matter how unlikely. For example, she recalls:

> Once, I remember I was in the bathtub, and I started thinking about how heavy bathtubs are when they're filled with water. I could convince myself that the bathtub was going to fall through the floor and that I was gonna be killed. I got out of the bathtub, and then it just made me laugh that I actually convinced myself that the bathtub was going to fall through the floor. But I really believed it. For a few seconds, I believed it.

Her upbringing as the only child of older, Depression-era parents shaped her view of the world as a scary place. They told her she had two jobs: do well in school and don't die. Death is the ultimate subject to worry about and the premise of some of her greatest cartoons.

But most of Chast's cartoons depict not death but the banality of life. These cartoons focus on the ordinary. Her characters often offer oddball observations. These scratchily drawn, couch-bound apartment-dwellers, posed against diamond-patterned wallpaper, live a life of chatty desperation.

A COLD WORLD: BRUCE ERIC KAPLAN

Known by his initials BEK, Bruce Eric Kaplan presents a world drained of warmth. Characters inhabit a glacial void, nominally defined by a sidewalk or generic interior. Eyes, normally a cartoon character's most expressive facial feature, are near-empty ovals. Even children bring no joy in BEKville. "Joy is not a fertile ground for humor," he observed.

There's no need to engage in armchair psychoanalyzing of Mr. Kaplan. He lays things out plainly in his memoir *I Was a Child*, a recollection of his youth that is both hilarious and heartbreaking. Recalling an incident when he fell asleep during nap time in kindergarten, he writes, "When I woke up, I was alone in an empty room, disoriented, seized with fear. It was as if I was the only person left on the planet. *No one else exists*, I thought. *Maybe I don't even exist anymore*."

Fear of abandonment haunted him as a boy. He imagined that his parents and brothers might sneak out of the house

when he was sleeping, and it wasn't until he heard them breathing in the next room that he could relax. Again in his memoir, he recalls that his favorite old movies on TV were "about how the person who was supposed to love you the most actually hated you enough to want you dead."

Kaplan's characters defy our expectations of parents, spouses, and others who are supposedly close to us. The humor derives from how blatantly and unapologetically these expressions of ambivalence or distrust are delivered. In discussing his cartoons, Kaplan confesses how deeply personal they are. "I put as much of myself as possible into my work," he has said. "My cartoons are me."

His cartoons venture into dark terrain, the thoughts that cross our minds when we are most upset and insecure. While such considerations remain in the shadows for most of us, BEK's world exists in sharply defined black and white. Notice the curious black bar on the right-side border of his cartoons; while Kaplan has no explanation other than "it just looks right," and "my hand did it, not my brain," perhaps it suggests something even darker looms beyond the panel.

Kaplan cites the surrealist painter Giorgio de Chirico as an influence, and it's easy to see why. The sharp shadows, abandoned plazas, and dark moodiness of de Chirico's paintings evoke the same existential feelings suggested in Kaplan's cartoons. As for Kaplan's comedic influence,

he acknowledges James Thurber, whose cartoons often convey an admixture of whimsy and social anxiety.

Despite being a well-respected cartoonist, who also found success as a TV writer and producer, Kaplan is haunted by what he describes as existential loneliness. "You can have love, companionship, kids, but you're still stuck in your head," he told us. Notwithstanding his accomplishments, Kaplan's basic personality infuses his cartoons. "We're born alone and we die alone."

All is not doom and gloom, however. Kaplan writes kids' books, too, and they're funny.

THE PESSIMIST: FRANK COTHAM

One of the *New Yorker*'s most prolific cartoonists for decades, Frank Cotham serves up a steady stream of bad news cartoons: doctors delivering bad prognoses, medieval castles under siege, and hillbillies observing the world from their ramshackle porch.

A cartoonist more at home in the quiet environs outside Memphis than in a big city, Cotham is an unfailingly polite, old-school cartoonist. Where the darkness comes from is not obvious, but as he readily admits, "I'm a 'glass is completely empty' sort of person. If anything's going to go wrong, it will, no matter what. I just try to see the humor in the really awful stuff that happens," he told us with a wicked laugh.

Not only is his humor dark, but the cartoons themselves are also dark, owing

"Unfortunately, there's no cure—there's not even a race for a cure."

to his heavy use of watercolor crayon. It gives his drawings "a murky texture that I kinda like," in his words. Even the gray and ominous clouds in his cartoons convey the message: there's no hope, but there is humor.

THE INTROVERT: LIANA FINCK

Some cartoonists rely on shocking images to convey a sense of the strange in their work. By contrast, Liana Finck presents cartoons that have an odd, fragile quality to them. The line in her drawing looks thin and quavery, the settings oddly barren, and the characters appear as flattened abstractions. Yet Finck's cartoons have a quiet power. They are like folded notes slipped anonymously under someone's door.

Finck recalled that she was a shy and self-conscious kid and that drawing was a way to connect with people and make friends. In art school she felt creatively blocked, believing that art had to be "holy." After a period of paralyzing self-criticism, Finck experienced a "feminist awakening," in her words. She freed herself from worshiping male artists to follow her own artistic path—although she has cited two male artists, Saul Steinberg and Brian Rae,

"I made you a vest."

among others, as influences on her work as a cartoonist.

Finck's cartoons evoke a sense of disconnect from reality, a private world where oddly funny things occur.

Cartoons are more a form of conscious self-expression for Finck than for other cartoonists. Once angry at the world, Finck has mellowed since her marriage and the birth of her child. She still draws as a way "to figure out how to exist in society." Not surprisingly for this introverted outsider, the title of her graphic memoir is *Passing for Human*.

THE STRANGE HOMEBODY: GEORGE BOOTH

A bare lightbulb dangling from the ceiling is the calling card of a singular cartoonist: George Booth. The characters illuminated by that bulb are generally crotchety oldsters muddling their way through their remaining years. They make odd pronouncements to spouses familiar with their peculiar ways. They are George Booth's people.

The most frequent setting of his cartoons is a simply furnished room with homey

"I'd just like to know what in hell is happening, that's all! I'd like to know what in hell is happening! Do you know what in hell is happening?"

comforts that bear an uncanny resemblance to his own household furnishings. A toothy mongrel with an insane expression often provides silent commentary.

Booth's rural Missouri upbringing gives a clue to the style of humor: These cartoons are not slickly sophisticated. They are little scenes of folks trying to make sense of the world. Booth peeks into windows and eavesdrops on the telling remarks of a house's inhabitants. The thin, scratchy line and casual ink wash give his work

an appropriately folksy, almost disheveled appearance. Yet his cartoons are carefully constructed and balanced.

DOMESTIC DISPUTANT: WILLIAM HAEFELI

William Haefeli's cartoons are notable for two things: their lush renderings, as previously discussed, and the everydayness of their scenarios. No monsters, space aliens, or cavemen appear in his cartoons. Instead, couples squabble, parents raise

"There's an article in here that explains why you're such an idiot."

children, and acquaintances engage in social jousting.

The characters are remarkably similar: well-educated, upper middle class, articulate, and assertive. They are both gay and straight. They speak their mind. The joke is not in the scene; it's in the perfectly rendered caption.

The subject of Haefeli's cartoons is relationships, whether social, parental, or spousal. The humor shares a sensibility with the comedy of manners, with its satirical but realistic look at social conventions. The comments are like clever lines in a play, and the characters unleash their critical judgments on others with civil hostility.

THE GENTLE TOUCH: AMY HWANG

At the opposite end of the spectrum from the angry, depressed, and neurotic cartoonists stands Amy Hwang. She depicts a world of relative tranquility, of kitties and coffee cakes, offering a gentle humor that tickles, not slaps. Her cartoons are more like pages from her diary, a glimpse into her daily world.

That's a bit of an oversimplification, of course. She reluctantly acknowledges the accuracy of that impression:

> I don't know if I really want to be the gentle person. There's the cartoonist you want to be, and then there's the cartoonist you are. You can't really change that. . . . It's

"I hope you sat me next to someone who wants to hear all about my bathroom renovation."

strange, because we all use humor when you're faced with some sort of miserable situation. I think that's how a lot of cartoonists became cartoonists. You use cartoons to cope with any sort of issues.

Her focus is on the hiccups of everyday life and often features women friends confiding in one another or making

observations. The scenes illustrate social interactions, and reveal how people connect or fail to connect with one another. The relationships among the speakers are close—everyone knows each other.

The line in Hwang's drawings is uniform, the washes varied, and the compositions direct—we always know where to look. Hwang's signature facial features comprise two dots for the eyes, a tiny, pointed projection for the nose, and a short slit or miniature oval for the mouth. Any interpersonal conflict, if it exists, is muted. The art pairs well with the understated humor.

SLICE OF MID-LIFE: VICTORIA ROBERTS

The cartoons of Victoria Roberts spring like flowers from the pages of the *New Yorker.* They brim with a childlike delight in the everyday. Roberts presents a joyful, uncomplicated world, free of cynicism and conflict.

Many of her cartoons feature just two characters: a balding, middle-aged man seated in a comfortable chair, and his exuberant wife, dressed in a wildly patterned dress that barely contains her bulbous body. She exclaims and he listens, as passive as one of their pet pugs. Indeed, he is often superfluous, there only to acknowledge his wife's oddball observations. The wife may have been inspired by Roberts' mother, whom she described as "a bit of a diva, a real character."

"I love drawing my couple who have been in a relationship for many, many years and can be funny without telling a joke,"

"Just reclaiming my Latino roots."

Roberts said in an interview. In that sense, her cartoons are akin to George Booth cartoons; both rely on domestic settings peopled by eccentric but likable characters, who make pronouncements to anybody who will listen.

Roberts' cartoons are like little domestic comedy scenes, featuring a strong female lead. There's no joke to "get"; her cartoons give pleasure for the sense of whimsy they evoke.

THE OUTRAGEOUS ONES
CROSSING THE LINE: EDWARD STEED

From the current generation of cartoonists, no one has left such an early, indelible mark as Edward Steed. His cartoon world teems with psychopaths doing horrible things. If a character is smiling, the smile is malevolent. Steed's humor goes beyond dark; it is savage. He slashes at accepted norms, revealing the disturbing tendencies we struggle to hide. His jagged line and spare

settings evoke a somewhat unformed but still recognizable world. This unassuming Englishman has no peer among his contemporaries in outrageous cartoon humor.

A psychologist would have a field day analyzing both the creator of such work and why we find his cartoons funny. As Steed has said, "Everything's kind of a glimpse of my subconscious. At times it's quite revealing, and I do hesitate sometimes." One may wonder what he hesitates to draw.

Violence or the threat of violence is a common theme, but the humor derives not from harmful acts but from the absurdity of the situations. The harshness is leavened by the unlikely depravity of his characters. A visit to the doctor's office, in real life, may provoke anxiety. A doctor with a good bedside manner recognizes it and prepares the patient psychologically for treatment. The assumptions go out the window if the physician is insane and the remedy involves boxes of bees.

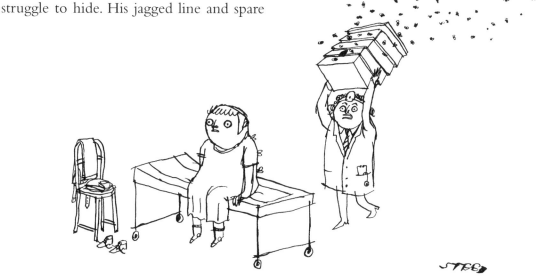

"This might sting a little."

Some may be repelled by his cartoons. They are at least as shocking as they are funny. The characters seem soulless. The humor pokes at our fears and vulnerabilities. The artwork is good enough to get the joke across and no better. But his darkly outrageous view of the world makes him the Voltaire of cartoonists.

HEART OF DARKNESS: GAHAN WILSON

Possibly more than any other influential cartoonist, Gahan Wilson relies on horror—really nightmarish stuff—in his cartoons. People show up in gruesome forms—often bloated, rubbery creatures with bulging eyes. Monsters that children imagine under their beds confront their adult selves. Despite the ghoulishness, loopy humor pervades Wilson's work. It's no wonder many cartoonists admire his work for its daring and meticulous craftsmanship.

At the beginning of his career, magazine editors were understandably reluctant to expose their readers to Wilson's

"Shouldn't Willis be in the bed and his imaginary monster under it?"

macabre imaginings. But soon he was given free creative rein at *Playboy* and later at *National Lampoon*, as well as more mainstream publications.

Wilson has said he constructs his cartoons as would a movie director. He takes into account the cast, script, lighting, set, atmosphere, and costumes. "I was a creepy little kid," he has confessed, devouring copies of *Weird Tales*, transfixed by 1950s monster movies. When a circus came to town, he dragged his father to see the freak shows. Later, he studied the scary-funny cartoons of Charles Addams and much admired their precision and dark atmosphere. But whereas Addams' world was largely confined to the dilapidated Victorian mansion that housed his characters, Wilson mixed the lurid with the everyday, creating a tension that underlies his humor.

Wilson's cartoons may suggest a creator with a dark soul, but Wilson was a gentle man, concerned with protecting the environment and saddened by human cruelty. "I love people," he said in an interview, "and I think it's such a terrible shame that we treat each other so badly that we hurt each other."

Some find his humor sick or at least distasteful, but Wilson's cartoons do not shock merely for the sake of shock. They shine a bright light on the unthinkable, and that tends to make us all a bit uncomfortable.

THE KING OF IRREVERENCE: SAM GROSS

Sam Gross had an extraordinary talent for telling a great joke in cartoon form. His humor runs the gamut from sick to tender. The characters range from stupid Nazis—one of his books is titled *We Have Ways of Making You Laugh: 120 Funny Swastika Cartoons*—to talking inanimate objects. Everything and everyone was gag-worthy, including the blind and disabled characters featured in his cartoon collection *I Am Blind and My Dog Is Dead*.

Gross was fearless in exposing the absurdities of life. He helped redefine what was acceptable, at least in some circles, to laugh at. The *National Lampoon*, where good taste was not a limiting factor, proved to be an ideal outlet, and he served as its cartoon editor for a time. On the next page, one of his best-known cartoons, published in that magazine, addresses man's inhumanity to frogs.

Gross never seemed to have experienced cartoonist's block. As noted earlier, his output over six decades exceeded 33,000 cartoons. By his estimate, he discarded 5,000 cartoons as obsolete or insufficiently funny—more than some cartoonists produce in a career. Some of his drawings look a bit tossed off, but he was known to take two or three weeks to get the image just right. His art style was simple and unadorned, "almost sweet," in the words of Michael Gerber, editor and publisher of *The*

S. GROSS

American Bystander—all the more surprising given his embrace of all that's irreverent.

Gross was modest about his artistic talents: "I don't consider myself a great artist, or even that much of a good artist, but what I consider myself is a really good gag man, a really good person that can tell a joke." The *New Yorker* agreed and published hundreds of his cartoons.

Cartoonists venerate Sam Gross. They admire his cartoons as simple, powerful missiles of humor. Few could match his ability to dream up scenarios that vary from the improbable to the impossible, twisting reality to fit the gag. He was a master of the craft.

Sam Gross, George Booth, and Gahan Wilson were titans of cartooning. Their prolific output and the world they represented—basically white, male, and mainstream—dominated gag cartoons. Magazine editors belatedly recognized that other viewpoints deserved attention, and actively cultivated a more diverse lineup of cartoonists that featured more women and more racial and ethnic minorities. In the next chapter, we'll explore how these outreach efforts have broadened the perspectives represented in the cartoon world.

CHAPTER TEN

Point of View

OTHER VOICES

Male sensibilities have dominated the world of humor since Aristophanes. The comedy tended toward rough, direct, and at someone else's expense. The delivery of the comedic material—whether on stage, radio, or in the movies—emphasized speed, timing, and a helpless target.

The world of cartooning exhibited the same influences. For decades, twentieth-century cartoons traded in scathing satire and merciless sendups. The cartoonist's personality stood in the shadows behind impersonal scenarios and punchlines. Occasionally women cartoonists' work appeared in magazines such as the *Saturday Evening Post* and *Collier's*, and a cartoon by Barbara Shermund ran in the very first issue of the *New Yorker* in 1925, but gag cartoons by women were the exception.

Sensibilities began changing as women entered the comedy arena in larger numbers in the 1960s. Female comics told stories instead of jokes, often directed their humor at themselves rather than others, and let the audience in on their lives. In the cartoon world, *New Yorker* cartoon editor Lee Lorenz took a chance on a young, shy artist who submitted intensely personal work. Beginning in 1978, with the acceptance of her first cartoon in that magazine, Roz Chast blazed a new comedic avenue for the next generation of cartoonists. She shared her life, anxieties, and neuroses in cartoons and books with an adoring readership. Over decades, the cocktail party zingers and clubby ripostes slowly gave way to cartoons about everyday observations and personal story-telling.

Bob Mankoff, who followed Lorenz as cartoon editor and who has contributed to three decades of *New Yorker* cartoons, summarizes this evolution in terms of "internal" versus "external," that is, personal versus impersonal:

When I look at men's and women's cartooning, I see differences as internal versus external. Overall, it seems to me that women, by culture—and maybe even by evolution—are more socially connected and have more empathy. Most humor doesn't care about those things. You wouldn't have known anything about Jack

Ziegler except that he was an interesting and imaginative guy. By contrast, when you look at a Roz Chast cartoon, you know a lot about Roz.

The concerns of women began moving to center stage in cartoons. Barbara Smaller, a keen observer of family life, noted the tectonic social shifts as women poured into the workforce. Her cartoons reflected the new realities of working moms, including exhaustion. As the feminist movement transfigured our society, female cartoonists were challenged to convey that new reality with humor. Smaller's strategy in her cartoon was to convert the tried and true "Not tonight honey" cliché into a statement both socio-political and wryly funny.

Emily Flake, perhaps more than any other cartoonist, has delivered hard truths in comic form about marriage and motherhood. Anger and frustration, tinged with elements of self-doubt and insecurity, permeate her cartoons. Underlying it all is a truth that justifies her grievances. The lady doth not protest too much.

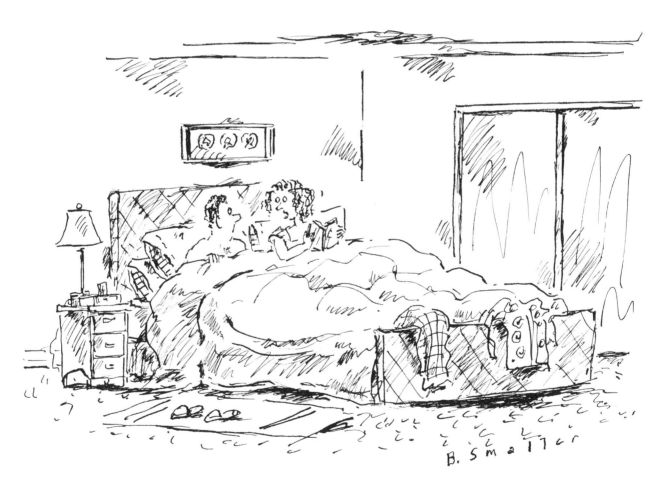

"Worse than a headache—I have three kids and a full-time job."

"Oh, there's your problem—twenty years of resentment at having to do the dishes."

adept at showing the subtleties and shading of these conversations but in a warmly comedic light. Amy Hwang allows us to eavesdrop on two women opining about life without a partner. Hwang's observation is equal parts sly and droll, with a soupçon of hard-won wisdom in the caption.

We're not saying that women cartoonists confine themselves to relationship issues or that men are incapable of a cartooning point-of-view that focuses on the internal. Too many counterexamples exist to allow for blanket statements. Bruce Kaplan's work, discussed in the previous chapter, is intensely personal. However, when shedding light on the single life, his humor style is far more rancorous than Hwang's, as Bob Mankoff noted:

Conversations between women, especially about delicate matters like relationships, are handled differently than men's competitive repartee. Female cartoonists are

"WHEN YOU'RE SINGLE, YOU'RE NEITHER LOVED NOR HATED."

If you compare Amy Hwang, who I brought into the *New Yorker*, and who's also a wonderful person, and Bruce Eric Kaplan, whose cartoons are also very much about what he's thinking, you see how much more aggressive Bruce's cartoons are. Amy's are sort of self-deprecating. In Bruce's cartoons, everybody wants to kill themselves just because how annoying everybody else is.

But which cartoon is funnier? Like any work of art, that judgment is in the eye of the beholder. We like them both.

Women cartoonists seem more comfortable opening up about deeper emotional levels. Ellie Black's cartoon on the following page aches with yearning and loneliness, hardly a wellspring of laughs. She eschews predictable bedtime fantasies by male cartoonists in favor of simple companionship. Our Netflix-watching single wants instant love in the Internet age without taking her eyes off her show—all without the hassle of dating. The gag is funny yet tinged with melancholy.

"Maybe I'm never going to find the person I'm supposed to do a real number on."

William Haefeli introduced readers of the *New Yorker* to gay and lesbian characters navigating the perils of everyday life from the non-straight point of view. While most of his cartoons don't relate to the concerns of the gay and lesbian populace, his cartoons serve as a reminder how underrepresented this group remains in cartoons. While Haefeli's point of view is clear, his cartoons often turn on the commonality between the straight world and the gay and lesbian community.

As a syndicated newspaper cartoonist, Hilary Price is more constrained in depicting lesbian characters in her daily feature *Rhymes With Orange*. Price may use the pronoun "they" when referring to a character's romantic partner, or avoid sexual orientation issues by substituting household pets for people, although a careful reader will make the connection. No such limitations apply to her identity as a Jewish cartoonist; she delights in giving Hanukkah and Passover comic treatment.

The concept of internal versus external can be stretched beyond gender to other characterizations that create distance between people. The term "otherness" refers to a sense of being apart from or not belonging to the dominant cultural group. In Western culture, the most obvious "other" groups comprise racial minorities.

"By the time we can marry in all fifty states, we'll probably be divorced."

The funny pages were once as white as the newspaper they were printed on, but now cartoon strips by Black cartoonists—primarily featuring Black characters—share the page with *Blondie* and other legacy strips. *Wee Pals* by Morrie Turner, the first nationally syndicated Black cartoonist, and *Curtis* by Ray Billingsley offered an inclusive take on race issues, paving the way for more pointed strips, such as Aaron McGruder's *The Boondocks* and Darrin Bell's *Candorville*. The multi-talented Bell also won a Pulitzer Prize for his editorial cartoons, a category unfortunately no longer recognized by the Pulitzer Prize Board. The prolific Keith Knight produces both *(Th)ink*, an editorial cartoon, and *The K Chronicles*, a light feature about his everyday life.

But none of those excellent cartoonists—and plenty of others we could list—create single-panel gag cartoons. Likewise, few Hispanic cartoonists work in this area. It's not the fault of magazine editors, who generally want to diversify the ranks of cartoonists. Indeed, women have served as cartoon editors at many top publications, including the *Wall Street Journal*, *Barron's*, *Playboy*, and the *New Yorker*. In particular, the *New Yorker* has made a concerted effort to embrace the work of the LGBTQ community, women, and people of color, giving a career boost to cartoonists who might not think to submit to the magazine. Among those who have benefited: Akeem Roberts, Victor Varnado, Liz Montague, Yasin Osman, Jerald Lewis II, and Lonny Milsap.

And, while not directly impacting the success of cartoonists of color, several magazine editors have told contributors that they want cartoons to include characters that reflect society's racial diversity. Not long ago, characters were white by default; and if a cartoon included a Black character, the gag turned on that racial distinction.

Everett (E. S.) Glenn, a Black American cartoonist currently residing in Berlin, doesn't place his racial identity at the center of his cartoons, although he often includes a cartoon version of himself in his work. Some of his cartoon characters are Black and others are not, but he doesn't shy away from subjects that underscore the "otherness" of being Black. A routine traffic stop is a common cartoon situation, but when the cop is white and the driver is Black, the humor angle narrows. Glenn puts the question usually spoken by the cop in the mouth of the driver, with a verbal twist that makes the point (see next page).

London-based artist Sarah Akinterinwa turned her artistic skills toward developing a series of single-panel cartoons around the lives of a young Black couple, "Oyin and Kojo." She developed the characters while unemployed during the Covid pandemic and posted a new cartoon every day on Instagram. They caught the attention of Emma Allen, the current cartoon editor at the *New Yorker*, who encouraged her to submit to the magazine. Akinterinwa sold one of the Oyin and Kojo cartoons with her very first submission. Prior to that, she hadn't even tried to sell her cartoons.

Her creation of Oyin and Kojo was a response to the absence of relatable characters who were people of color, especially in the U.K. "I can't think of many positive examples of Black couples in media to look to," she told us. "And in cartoons, I can't think of many Black couple characters."

Courtesy of Sarah Akinterinwa.

"Give me one week to cultivate
the perfect comeback to the point you just made!"

"Any idea why you pulled me over today, officer?"

So she created them. Her cartoons present a normal, funny couple, who happen to be Black, going about their everyday lives. By not making racial issues central to her cartoons, she feels she is "normalizing Black people as characters," in her words. "When I wake up in the morning, I don't think to myself, how can I have a great Black day?" she said with a laugh. At the same time, she stressed the importance of including a racially and ethnically diverse cast of cartoon characters. "My intention always is to think of even the least represented people."

"Notice how the table is round, so that everyone sitting at it is equal."

Efforts to diversify the workplace can itself can be the target of satire. The seemingly well-meaning but tone-deaf white guy invites the cartooning treatment, and Jeremy Nguyen obliges with this take on the corporate meeting. Nice try, Mr. Stuffed Suit, but we know who holds the power to hire and fire.

Epilogue

The Rockies may crumble, Gibraltar may tumble, but cartoons are here to stay. They endure because they delight. The best of them bend our brain waves to their will, offering us a worldview through the cartoonist's cracked prism. Reality is recognized but rearranged to make a certain cartoon sense.

Felipe Galindo-Feggo had the right idea: cartoons can bring contentment. Substitute the ubiquitous palm tree on a desert island with a potted palm atop a stack of books, and new life is breathed into a hoary cartoon setup. No words are needed. We leave the reader—both you and the cartoon character—to enjoy more funny stuff.

Appendix A
TOP 100 CARTOON CLICHÉS

Aliens encounter Earthlings

Ascent of Man evolution illustration

Astronomer in observatory

Beached whale

Big fish chasing little fish

Botticelli's *Birth of Venus*

Bride and groom at altar

Building the Egyptian pyramids

Business executive pointing to sales chart

Car salesman and customer

Cat versus mouse

Cave paintings

Chalk outlines at crime scenes

Chicken versus egg

Clergyman delivering eulogy

Cloud-watching and identifying

Clowns in tiny car

Comedy and tragedy masks

Complaint window

Couple caught cheating in bed

Couples counselor with couple

Crash-test dummies

Crawling through desert

Creation of Frankenstein's monster

Damsels in distress

Desert island

Dinosaurs and killer meteor

Discovery of fire

Doctor delivering bad news

Duelists

Dungeon prisoners

Easter Island heads

Emergency mid-flight announcement

Engraving on tombstone(s)

Explorers in quicksand

Fish evolving into land creature

Fortune-teller and customer

Funeral parlor viewing

Galley slaves

General pointing to service ribbons

Genie granting wishes

Godzilla destroying city

Good cop, bad cop

Guru on mountain

Guy in stocks

Halloween trick-or-treaters

Headless praying mantis

Hibernating bears

Ice hole fishing

Igloos

Invention of the wheel

IRS auditor and taxpayer

Jester trying to entertain king

Kids building sandcastles

Lab rat in maze

Last words on deathbed

Lawyer arguing to judge or jury

Lawyer reading will

Lemmings

Lost and Found window

Marriage proposal

Maternity ward

Men's club codgers

Michelangelo's God creating Adam

Military round table

Mobsters and victim at pier

Mount Rushmore variations

Munch's *The Scream*

Noah's Ark

Optometrist and eye chart

Ostrich with head in sand

Parent reading bedtime story

Patent office

Patient on examining table

Patient on psychiatrist's couch

Perusing books by genre in bookstore

Police lineup

Politician delivering stump speech

Prisoners counting the days with marks on wall

Realtor showing homes for sale

Road signs

Rodin's *The Thinker*

Russian nesting dolls

Scientists with equations on blackboards

Selecting a greeting card

Snow globe variations

Star constellations

Stonehenge

Surgical team in operating theater

The damned in hell

The End-Is-Nigh Guy

The Last Supper

Traffic cop pulling over speeding motorist

Trojan horse

Tunnel of Love

TV news and weather

Viewing modern art in museum

Walking the plank

Witch stirring cauldron

Yoga class

You-are-here map

Appendix B
CHARACTERS WE KNOW AND (MOSTLY) LOVE

BIBLICAL

Adam and Eve

Four Horsemen of the Apocalypse

God

Jesus

Moses

Noah

Saint Peter

Satan

FAIRYTALES, FOLKTALES, NURSERY RHYMES

Cinderella

Gingerbread Man

Goldilocks and the Three Bears

Grim Reaper

Hansel and Gretel

Humpty Dumpty

Jack and the Beanstalk

Little Red Riding Hood and the Big, Bad Wolf

Old woman who lived in a shoe

Pinocchio

Rapunzel

Robin Hood

Santa Claus

Sleeping Beauty

Snow White and the Seven Dwarves

The Little Engine That Could

The Three Little Pigs and the Big, Bad Wolf

The Tortoise and the Hare

Vampires

HISTORICAL

Abraham Lincoln

America's Founding Fathers

Christopher Columbus

Einstein

Joan of Arc

King Arthur and Knights of the Round Table

Napoleon

Shakespeare

LITERARY

Moby-Dick and Ahab

Wizard of Oz characters

MYTHICAL

Abominable Snowman

Atlas

Centaurs

Cupid

Medusa

Sisyphus

Unicorns

Zeus

OTHER

Cavemen and cavewomen

Comic book superheroes

Magritte's "self-portrait" with apple

Pirates

Illustration Credits

Page	Artist	Source
Cover	Mick Stevens	CartoonStock
v	Benjamin Schwartz	Courtesy of Benjamin Schwartz
vi	Sam Gross	CartoonStock
x	Mick Stevens	CartoonStock
2	P. C. Vey	CartoonStock
3	Jack Ziegler	CartoonStock
4	Eric Lewis	CartoonStock
5	Carolita Johnson	CartoonStock
6	Bob Mankoff	CartoonStock
7	Joe Dator	CartoonStock
8	Joe Dator	CartoonStock
9	Bob Mankoff	CartoonStock
12	Paul Noth	CartoonStock
14	Edward Koren	CartoonStock
15	David Borchart	CartoonStock
16	John O'Brien	CartoonStock
17	Arnie Levin	CartoonStock
18	Trevor Spaulding	CartoonStock
19	Edward Steed	CartoonStock
20	P. C. Vey	CartoonStock
21	Bob Mankoff	CartoonStock

Page	Artist	Source
22	Sam Gross	CartoonStock
23	Tom Toro	CartoonStock
25	David Sipress	CartoonStock
26	Edward Steed	CartoonStock
27	Mick Stevens	CartoonStock
28	Roz Chast	Courtesy of Roz Chast
30	Kaamran Hafeez	Courtesy of Kaamran Hafeez
31 (top)	Kaamran Hafeez	Courtesy of Kaamran Hafeez
31 (bottom)	Kaamran Hafeez	Courtesy of Kaamran Hafeez
32	Kaamran Hafeez	Courtesy of Kaamran Hafeez
33 (top)	Kaamran Hafeez	CartoonStock
33 (bottom)	Frank Cotham	CartoonStock
35 (top)	John O'Brien	Courtesy of John O'Brien
35 (bottom)	John O'Brien	Courtesy of John O'Brien
36	John O'Brien	CartoonStock
37	Bob Mankoff	CartoonStock
39	Roz Chast	CartoonStock
41	Jack Ziegler	CartoonStock
43	Sofia Warren	CartoonStock
44	Mick Stevens	CartoonStock
45	Elisabeth McNair	CartoonStock
46	Michael Crawford	CartoonStock
47 (top)	Paul Noth	CartoonStock
47 (bottom)	Ellis Rosen	CartoonStock
48	Victoria Roberts	CartoonStock
49 (top)	Anonymous	Courtesy of Frank Cotham
49 (bottom)	Frank Cotham	CartoonStock
50 (top)	Kaamran Hafeez	CartoonStock
50 (bottom)	Kaamran Hafeez	Courtesy of Kaamran Hafeez
51	Marisa Acocella	CartoonStock
54	Kim Warp	CartoonStock
55	Robert Weber	CartoonStock
56	Julia Suits	CartoonStock
57	Leo Cullum	CartoonStock
58	Benjamin Schwartz	CartoonStock
59	Pat Byrnes	CartoonStock

Page	Artist	Source
60 (top)	Shannon Wheeler	CartoonStock
60 (bottom)	Liam Walsh	CartoonStock
61	Jason Patterson	CartoonStock
64	Jason Adam Katzenstein	CartoonStock
65	Harry Bliss	CartoonStock
66	William Hamilton	CartoonStock
67	Victoria Roberts	CartoonStock
68	P. C. Vey	CartoonStock
69	Teresa Burns Parkhurst	CartoonStock
70	Frank Cotham	CartoonStock
71	Leo Cullum	CartoonStock
72	Jack Ziegler	CartoonStock
75	Julia Suits	CartoonStock
76	William Haefeli	CartoonStock
77	Phil Witte	CartoonStock
78	Sam Gross	CartoonStock
79	J. C. Duffy	CartoonStock
80	P. C. Vey	CartoonStock
81	Christopher Weyant	CartoonStock
82	Kim Warp	CartoonStock
83	Mick Stevens	CartoonStock
84 (top)	John Jonik	CartoonStock
84 (bottom)	Joe Dator	CartoonStock
85	John O'Brien	CartoonStock
86 (top)	Liana Finck	CartoonStock
86 (bottom)	Seth Fleishman	CartoonStock
88	Jack Ziegler	CartoonStock
89	James Thurber	CartoonStock
90	Michael Maslin	Courtesy of Michael Maslin
91 (top)	Barbara Smaller	CartoonStock
91 (bottom)	Charles Barsotti	CartoonStock
92	Charles Addams	The Tee and Charles Addams Foundation
93	Lee Lorenz	CartoonStock
94	Robert Weber	CartoonStock
95	William Haefeli	CartoonStock
97	Drew Dernavich	CartoonStock

Page	Artist	Source
98	Phil Witte	CartoonStock
100	Saul Steinberg	The Saul Steinberg Foundation / Artists Rights Society (ARS)
102	Roz Chast	CartoonStock
103	Bruce Kaplan	CartoonStock
105	Frank Cotham	CartoonStock
106	Liana Finck	CartoonStock
107	George Booth	CartoonStock
108	William Haefeli	CartoonStock
109	Amy Hwang	CartoonStock
110	Victoria Roberts	CartoonStock
111	Edward Steed	CartoonStock
112	Gahan Wilson	CartoonStock
114	Sam Gross	CartoonStock
116	Roz Chast	CartoonStock
117	Barbara Smaller	CartoonStock
118 (top)	Emily Flake	CartoonStock
118 (bottom)	Amy Hwang	CartoonStock
119	Bruce Kaplan	CartoonStock
120	Ellie Black	CartoonStock
121	William Haefeli	CartoonStock
122	Sarah Akinterinwa	Courtesy of Sarah Akinterinwa
123	E. S. Glenn	CartoonStock
124	Jeremy Nguyen	CartoonStock
125	Felipe Galindo-Feggo	CartoonStock

About the Authors

Phil Witte is a cartoonist and author. His cartoons have appeared in dozens of publications in the United States and United Kingdom, including the *Wall Street Journal*, *Barron's*, *Reader's Digest*, *Private Eye*, the *New Statesman*, and, as a collaborator, the *New Yorker*. Phil's work has been exhibited in galleries in the United States and Europe. He wrote two joke books on aging, *What You Don't Know About Turning 50* and the sequel on turning 60, and has contributed humor pieces to print and online publications. Phil has also written straight articles and essays for the *Washington Post*, *Chicago Tribune*, and other leading newspapers. He was a cartoonist-in-residence at the Charles Schulz Museum and the San Francisco Cartoon Art Museum. He's a member of the National Cartoonists Society, and a lawyer to boot. See www.philwitte.com and https://www.instagram.com/philwitte cartoons. Phil lives with his wife Rebecca in the San Francisco Bay Area.

Rex Hesner is a jazz musician, writer, and cartoon critic. He established *Cartoon Companion*, arguably the world's first website dedicated to reviewing and rating single-panel cartoons. He and collaborator Phil Witte wrote weekly postings over a two-year period before attracting the attention of *New Yorker* cartoon editor, Bob Mankoff. Migrating to Mankoff's online cartoon treasure trove, CartoonStock.com, provided Rex and Phil with half a million cartoons to feed their semi-monthly thematic blog, *Anatomy of a Cartoon*. Over 100 blog posts later, they're still at it. Rex lives with his wife Susan on the San Francisco waterfront.